Praise for *The Accidental Farmers*

"Tim Young has written a maddeningly enchanting description of how he and his wife Liz decided to dump their successful careers in the corporate world and seek a simpler life of organic farming in harmony with nature. With wit, humor and precision, Tim mesmerizes the reader as he and Liz learn how to achieve a life of harmony with the natural world. I promise you a compellingly delightful read."
—**Mildred Armstrong Kalish, author of** *Little Heathens* (*New York Times Book Review* "**One of the 10 Best Books of 2007**").

"Tim and Liz Young describe the many benefits of a return to agrarian life, one of which is a return to vibrant health; because the nutrient-dense meat, fat and organ meats of animals fed on fertile soil is the absolute basis of human health and fertility. In a most compelling way, they present that beautiful equation: healthy soil equals healthy animals equals healthy human beings."
—**Sally Fallon Morell, author of** "**Nourishing Traditions**" **and President of the Weston A. Price Foundation**

"You may have successful job or career but perhaps you are bored to death with it now and looking for something more challenging. If you have always been attracted to rural life, this book is made for you! Tim and Liz Young recount the joys and sorrows along with the victories and defeats of finding success in one of the most challenging professions; not just farming but also farming a totally natural way. I particularly recommend their thoughts on the 'dark side of farming' and Tim's very well reasoned discussion of what financial profit means in farming."
—**Gene Logsdon, author of many books including** *The Contrary Farmer, Holy Shit: Managing Manure to Save Mankind,* **and the novel** *Pope Mary and the Church of Almighty Good Food*

The
ACCIDENTAL
FARMERS

An Urban Couple, a Rural Calling
and a Dream of Farming in
Harmony with Nature

Tim Young

Harmony Publishing Company

First Edition

Library of Congress Cataloging-in-Publication Data is available upon request

ISBN 978-0-9832717-0-3

This book is dedicated to family

*To my mother for answering the phone at work and patiently
explaining how to separate an egg to a curious teenage boy with a
cookbook, thus igniting a lifelong interest in cooking.*

*To Brian and Sue for being model parents, great friends,
and bestowing upon the world a wonderful gift.
Namely, their daughter and my wife, Liz.*

*To Liz, the most beautiful soul I have ever known and my cherished
partner for every step taken on this journey through life.*

Acknowledgements

On the farm there are no days off, making it difficult to find time to rest, let alone write a book. This book was made possible in large part due to the support of two wonderful on-farm apprentices who handled many of the farm chores, giving me a few moments here and there to stare at the screen. To Kerry and Amanda, thank you for being so loving to our animals, for the respect you show the land and for the support you constantly gave to Liz and me throughout this project.

I also owe a big debt of gratitude to Evan Strome, who took the time to read large parts of this manuscript and provide insightful, candid feedback that shaped the outcome of this book.

To my wife Liz, who aided my recollection of key events, corrected some of my bizarre spelling habits and tirelessly knitted away while I typed away, giving me the freedom to finish this project that I accidentally began. No person could dream for a better partner in life.

Table of Contents

Only he can understand what a farm is, what a country is, who shall have sacrificed part of himself to his farm or country, fought to save it, struggled to make it beautiful. Only then will the love of farm or country fill his heart.

—Antoine de Saint-Exupery

Prologue

On a steamy August afternoon in a remote Georgia town, a rusted Ford station wagon fishtails up a long gravel drive, taking a mail carrier a mile off his scheduled route. The car stops in a cloud of dust before a farmhouse nestled high on a hill. The driver surveys the scene.

A large white house is surrounded by weathered farm equipment. To the right of the house a bountiful garden is eclipsed by an old yellow dump truck, the bed of which overflows with busted pallets, worn-out garden tools and shards of twisted metal. High above, five remarkably huge buzzards dive in a hypnotic Cirque du Soleil dance that captures the driver's attention as he exits the car. With a watchful eye on the sky, he retrieves a package from the rear, closes the door and wipes his brow. As he turns, four massive white dogs—born only with the instinct to viciously repel intruders—charge and announce his arrival with ferocious barking.

Agitated that I must stop working, I rush over to greet him, momentarily forgetting that my face is dripping with sweat and spattered with fresh blood.

The mailman opens his mouth to find that a parched, dry throat holds his words hostage. Shifting his weight nervously, he eyes the dogs whose mouths, he now observes, are also covered with blood.

Without uttering a word, I sign for the package with my bloodstained right hand as he stares at the razor-sharp knife held firmly in my left. He looks away and pretends to not notice the fragments of viscera that cling to my shirt. Surrounded by snarling dogs and a pungent smell the mailman realizes that he's come at a very bad time.

It's Wednesday, and I am killing chickens today.

Sometimes I wonder how on earth I got to this point in my life. Four years ago I collected frequent flyer miles, donned business suits, lived in lavish hotels, negotiated multi-million dollar deals, and knew not the first thing about farming. Now, four very long years later, I can't seem to recall that time.

Before farming, my life had a comfortable predictability to it. I had been flying high on a trajectory of success since entering the corporate world at the age of eighteen. Although golf was my first passion and I dreamed of becoming a professional golfer, life had another plan. During my first year of college I was lured into a minimum-wage warehouse job. I quit school, and without looking back I eagerly joined the rat race and sprinted unabated for the next twenty-five years. Along the way I rose to president of a division of a Fortune 500 company before starting my own business, a company that grew so rapidly that *Inc. Magazine* recognized it as one of America's fastest-growing businesses.

Then, for no apparent reason, but for many profound ones, I left it all behind. I quit that life—traded it in and put everything on the line—all to become a farmer.

The change was quite spontaneous, something uneventful at the time in my mind yet something of a shock to anyone who knew me, especially since I didn't grow up on a farm. True, I had lived in the country for a time as a child, but never on a farm. Indeed, for the first forty-five years of my life farms were nothing more than abstractions to me, something innately comprehensible yet completely foreign at the same time. They were expansive background areas I took little notice of while driving through the countryside as I inhaled fast-food, surfed channels on the satellite radio or, embarrassingly, read emails on my Blackberry.

On occasion I would observe livestock lingering on farms, teasing me with a sense of connection to cows that was akin to my relationship with clouds. Something I could see so it must be real but something that I had never touched so maybe it wasn't. Other farms showcased a single crop as far as I could tell but if the crop wasn't corn, it was alien to me. It could have been tobacco just as easily as collards. Beyond this fast-moving glimpse, I had no concept of their world, whoever these farmers were, and suspect they had no interest in mine. I bought food from a store not from a farmer, and most of what I saw while whizzing down the road bore no resemblance to the food I saw in the store.

The rat race I so eagerly embraced mandated extensive travel, which, having been raised in the mountains of north Georgia and having seen next to nothing of the world, was a requirement I longed to embrace. Traveling far and wide I relished in exotic local delicacies such as mooncakes in Singapore, haggis in Scotland, beignets in New Orleans, and Yorkshire pudding in London, which, I was astonished to learn, isn't pudding at all. Or at least nothing like the boxed pudding we ate for dessert in north Georgia, which more often than not followed a supper featuring Spam. Despite these culinary indulgences I rarely gave food a second thought and certainly never thought about where it came from. Why should I have?

Like everyone else I was surrounded by supermarkets, food warehouses, restaurants, fast-food joints and convenience stores, all of which offered a limitless selection of edible substances that I considered to be food. No matter where I was, if it was the middle of the night and everything was closed, no worries, as I could find something salty, sweet, chocolaty or crunchy in a vending machine, along with an ageless beverage to wash it down. My definition of local food was food that we could eat within a few minutes of the house. Never mind that the food traveled thousands of miles to get to us. If it was down the street at Kroger, Shaw's, Publix or Safeway, it was local. It wasn't my fault that I saw the world this way. I was simply a product of my environment.

My mother and her mother before her were wonderful home cooks. I mean real southern cooks, the kind who can make what we now label as "comfort food"—meals out of anything lying around the kitchen. We didn't call it comfort food back then. We called it food. Everyone knew what food was but somehow over the next few decades the definition would become purposefully obfuscated by clever marketers (their fault) preying on consumers who demanded cheap and fast sustenance and didn't care to know where it came from (our fault). Both my mother and grandmother were the kind of cooks—no, homesteaders, in my grandmother's case—who knew how to grow, can, render and preserve food so that they could feed us throughout the year. For centuries life-sustaining skills such as these were passed from one generation to the next. Now, remarkably, many of these most basic skills—how to preserve and prepare food—have been abdicated, delegated and very nearly lost.

Both ladies innately knew the ratios to make sauces, pastries, dough or what have you, and I took for granted then the ease with which they so deliciously fed us, the same way I eventually grew to take for granted the convenience of the foodstuffs that enveloped me some forty years later. Naturally growing up in the environment of such wonderful cooks encouraged me to be not only very comfortable in the kitchen, but instilled in me a lifelong interest in cooking.

And so it was rather alarming to me when I began to look closely at my life a few years ago only to discover how little cooking I was actually doing. Why was that?

The most obvious answer was that since prepared food was so plentiful and affordable there really was no reason to cook. The convenient access to food is why I waited until so late in the day before finally asking myself, "I wonder what's for dinner?" As I began to reflect on my cooking habits I also examined other areas of my life. Peeling back the layers of the life I had comfortably fallen into I also realized that there was no reason for me to change the oil in our car, since someone else could do that without me having to get dirty. The same was true with washing the car, so I often availed myself of the car-wash services available. Ditto for mowing the lawn, painting the house, repairing plumbing, installing electrical outlets, and countless other tasks that everyone likely did for himself a half century ago. These skills are all easily within reach of most of us and they were certainly within my reach. Yet how many people handle these tasks themselves versus hiring a contractor today? Is it that we all can't do them or do we simply tell ourselves "I don't have the time"? If the answer is the latter then why don't we? Are we are all working so hard to earn money to pay for food, housing, and other things that, if we weren't working so hard, we could grow, build, and provide for ourselves?

In rural America, as I've now learned, these tasks are handled routinely by individuals who are equally comfortable as welders, mechanics, or at giving one another hair cuts. Urban life, on the other hand, is far more specialized, with people having essentially one or two things to do, usually working at specific careers and, if they have them, attending to children. If they don't have children there's always spectator sports, concerts, dining, golf, museums, or some hobby/distraction that one can become immersed in—and spend a small fortune on.

Before farming I was lured by these distractions. I was a scratch (zero handicap) golfer and a huge pro football fan (go Steelers!). In some years we would attend ten concerts. Now I haven't touched a golf club in over five years and unless it's the Super Bowl rarely know if the Steelers won, let alone watch a game.

There's no time for such silliness when you're a farmer.

Even though my wife and I had the time, we found ourselves preparing less and less of our food, allowing ourselves to become seduced by the convenience of having someone else cook (and therefore clean up) for us. Indeed, for most people cooking is among the tasks that get in the way, and it's easier to not cook. All we needed to worry about was earning enough money to pay for the conveniences. Ah, but worry we did, for if the stock market dropped so did our perception of value and feeling of security. Overnight, like everyone else, we became, somehow, worth less than were just a few hours before. The pendulum swung both ways, for if the financial or real estate markets soared the commensurate increase in our 401K or home value would make us feel better off. But we weren't better off, anymore than the employees of Enron were a few years before when they thought their 401K and retirement plans were safe and secure. The Enron example was just one of many, along with countless financial bailouts, that disgusted me with much of the effect that government and corporate America has on so many individual's and family's lives. It added to the questions I had about what I was really doing with *my* life and whether it had *purpose*.

Unquestionably, before we became farmers, life seemed easier. It was a time when we had access to cable TV, paved driveways, convenient restaurants, and weekends off. Ironically though, life was also much *more* stressful then. Like most people we didn't question much and simply repeated each day what we did the day before.

Today I observe cows, sheep, rabbits, turkeys, pigs, and other animals, none of which give a hoot about the economy. What concerns them is whether or not they have grass, water, shade, safety, and companionship, which is all they ever care about. They feel no need to conquer the world or to climb Maslow's pyramid. In their natural environments they know why they are here and what they are supposed to do. They're grounded and connected with what life is really all about. They're content.

I wasn't.

Back then, in 2006, I knew nothing of their world. I had never touched a cow, sat on a tractor or plowed a field. I had worked in a suit my whole life but, upon reflection, couldn't put my finger on what I had really done. Was this all there was?

Work, make money and spend it? That's it? I think I knew all along that something was missing. I just never had the time to stop and ponder what it was. And so I can only wonder now what I would have said then had I been told that within four years there would be no more cubicles, conference calls or board meetings. Instead I would be raising, killing and butchering chickens, turkeys, geese, ducks, pigs, sheep, and cows.

Had someone suggested to me that rather than jet-setting I would be milking cows and making farmstead cheese from raw milk, or that my wife Liz and I would be making our own soap, bacon and lard while tanning hides, and growing, canning and preserving our own fruit and vegetables, how would I have reacted?

And if they went so far as to predict that we would be teaching others to do the same, fulfilling their own buried desires to reconnect with the origins of their food, I suspect my reply would have been tersely incredulous. "Why in the world would we do that?" That would indeed have been a sensible reply. With so much food available and such little thought or effort required to acquire it, why would we care about farming or producing food? What could possibly compel us to leave the comfort and security of our sheltered life to do something so outlandish—so risky—something so far removed from anything we had ever known?

And that's where this story begins.

PART 1

❧

Birth of a Farm

CHAPTER 1

An Awakening

When I was five years old my kindergarten teacher asked each child in the class what they wanted to be when they grew up. Of course this elicited many of the responses one would expect. A football player. A fireman. A doctor. One kid even dreamed of becoming a fireworks launcher.

"What do you want to become when you grow up, Tim?" Mrs. Jacobs asked, firmly putting me on the spot.

My eyes grew large. For a kid the options were endless. I loved sports and I loved superheroes like Batman and Robin. Maybe I could even be an actor! Here was my chance to become the coolest kid at Lollipop Lane kindergarten! Instead I blurted out my secret aspiration at the time.

"I want to be a florist!" I replied enthusiastically.

My response puzzled Mrs. Jacobs but she didn't show it. "How exciting!" she said, before probing deeper. "You want to arrange flowers?"

I stared pensively, processing her question and formulating the best reply my five-year-old vocabulary could muster.

"No! A florist! I want to put floors in houses!" I stammered. I suspect my infatuation with installing floors had something to do with all the bulldozers and carpenters I had been watching build my uncle's new house at the time. Mrs. Jacobs gently corrected my misunderstanding and explained that perhaps I wished to become a floor installer rather than a florist. Yet it seems that I may have been destined all along to take a long and winding road to my dream job.

Four decades passed all too quickly, lost in a whirlwind of perpetual hustle bustle in search of my calling. I never did become a floor installer, or a florist, for that matter. I zoomed through corporate America at high altitude and along the way lost a figurative and literal connection with the ground. I think I must have known it was happening all along, which explains the frequent camping and annual hunting trips I would take to reconnect with nature.

When I was twenty-one I had moved from Georgia to Massachusetts as part of a job transfer. I say that so matter-of-factly now, but the decision to move out of my mother's house, quit my secure job in Atlanta and move to where it's wicked cold and where I knew precisely no one was quite stressful at the time. Somehow I endured the ordeal and spent over twenty years in Massachusetts, learning to drop my "r's" while discovering that there was actually quite remarkable seafood beyond catfish and hushpuppies.

Throughout my life there have been so many seemingly insignificant steppingstones I have navigated and paths I have chosen that ultimately defined the kind of man I have become. I now know that making that decision to move was one of those for me. It was a hurdle to overcome and clearing it began the process of building my confidence when faced with difficult choices. This confidence would grow and allow me to summon the courage to later leave the security of a corporate paycheck for the scary uncertainty of starting my own business. Later it would give me the courage to start a farm.

I understood corporate America well enough. Indeed, after dropping out of college I had somehow climbed to president of a division of a Fortune 500 company when I was only twenty-five, a position I held for eight years. At thirty-four I walked away from the security of that job, faced my own fears and bootstrapped a one-person company that grew to 450 employees five years later. These "accomplishments" are supposed to make you feel good. They left me longing for something real, something more than a trophy. Something fulfilling.

I had learned how money was made and was disheartened by the fact that the jobs that really seem important to our collective welfare (which, coincidentally, are also the easiest to describe) are the ones that pay the least. I include police officers, fireman, social workers and teachers in there right along with farmers. Where would we be without them?

The jobs that are impossibly difficult to describe (imagine describing to a kindergarten class the job of an investment banker specializing in exotic financial instruments) are the ones deemed by capitalism to be most worthy of financial reward. Why is an *average* investment banker rewarded with social and financial perquisites at levels unattainable by the best firefighter who saves lives, or the greatest teacher who unleashes potential that would otherwise remain forever trapped? The world had become so much about money and influence, and both were concentrated in the hands of corporate and government powers.

In retrospect I suppose it was easy for me to leave the so-called glory to other people but I now longed to find my place in the world more than ever—something that made a difference while allowing me to earn a living. Something that was "real."

On October 12, 2006 it happened, and my path in life changed. My calling grew weary of waiting for me to find it and so it came looking for me. Other than being my wife Liz's birthday, there was nothing remarkably special about that day. There was certainly no "sign" that we would soon trade our safe and secure life on a half-acre lot in a suburban Atlanta golf community for a barren seventy-two-acre parcel two hours away without any notion of how to earn a living. We had never even discussed the possibility.

To celebrate her birthday the prior year, Liz and I had taken a weekend jaunt to St. Thomas, one of our favorite places in the world. "Jaunt"—now there's a word that, since I became a farmer, has been completely purged from my vocabulary. But before farming it wasn't only in my vocabulary, it was a reality. The plan for this birthday was to rise early, leave our manicured community behind and head for a local horseback-riding ranch. As always, we began the day by cooking nothing, opting instead to stop for something we could eat on the way. Starbucks won the coin toss that day with a venti latte and blueberry scone fueling our trip to the ranch.

I had never been riding with Liz and had barely ever ridden at all myself, but we both love nature and are crazy about animals, so I figured she'd like it. Lenny, Jack, and Polly, our three Labrador retrievers, tagged along to play with other dogs on the ranch, so the day was off to a great start. As we arrived at the ranch, Liz lit up when she saw the horses! As for me—well, let's just say that I was more comfortable with airplanes than horses.

Riding a horse in a wooded, natural setting like that, particularly since I was a novice, allowed me to experience a range of emotions that were completely foreign to me. My first thought was on mechanics—staying on the horse and keeping my balance. Always confident on the exterior, inside I was mildly terrified that the horse may take off on a wild tear (as they do in western movies) and I'd have no way of stopping him. Thankfully the horse chosen for me that day was more interested in napping than galloping, a mood that I shared and for which I was grateful as I walked him around the practice ring to get comfortable. Similar to skiing the "bunny trail," once I achieved a level of comfort I fell into a relaxed, almost giddy state. Then, I let go and began to feel.

Heading out onto the trail I began to notice the rhythm of the horse—the breathing, the sheer strength, and the graceful motion. I could feel the rocks, the gullies, and the soft and hard dirt that the horse felt. I wondered if it hurt the horse's hooves and I felt concern. A light breeze kissed my cheek and it had a sweetness coming from the flora that surrounded me. I wasn't used to this and as I rode, it caused me to ponder if there really was sweetness in the air, or if it was simply a lack of pollutants that made the air seem more sweet and fresh to me. I gradually and blissfully became intoxicated.

In an instant the sweetness was removed from the air as my horse had what I as a city slicker referred to as a bowel movement. I wasn't used to this either! Nor did I know if this was somehow a reflection on me and if I should excuse myself to the other riders. I said nothing. Years later, as a farmer I rarely even notice this but if I do I am thankful for the black gold that enriches the soil and makes life possible. But not that day.

I felt the horse's sweat and became connected to the land and my surroundings in a way that felt peculiar. My senses were heightened and I picked up on movements, as my peripheral vision seemed to expand like pupils in dim light. Birds, squirrels, blowing leaves, lizards—nothing escaped my visual acuity. As I continued my slow and steady ride along a densely wooded trail my attention turned to a stream that flowed gently over mountain rocks. I couldn't see it. I heard it. This made me aware of sounds, or more accurately the absence of sounds. There were no cars, no radios, no horns, no planes and no ambulances. There were no sounds of man, only the sounds that preceded man, and the sounds that will likely succeed him.

The sound of the horse's hooves seemed almost deafening but, strangely, in a comforting way. Thump, thump, thump. The sound made sense to me and I was viscerally connected through the horse's legs and hooves to Mother Earth. As the ride came to an end I dismounted and gently stroked the horse as if to say thank you. And indeed I was thankful, only I couldn't put my finger on what I was thankful for. Something inside me just felt right. I was enraptured and wondered if I had ever felt that content.

It was great fortune that Liz's birthday was in October, coinciding with apple season. Being a native New Englander from Massachusetts, Liz has a special fondness for fall. Having lived half of my life and all of my adult life in Massachusetts I had observed that most New Englanders share this feeling. And for good reason, for I have traveled nowhere that can match the quaint, homey feelings of Vermont and New Hampshire in October, not to mention the unsurpassed fall foliage put on display every year without fail. When Liz and I had moved to Georgia just two years prior, we sacrificed that crisp autumn air and traded it for an unfailingly beautiful southern springtime, which rarely makes an appearance in Massachusetts. We figured the harsh winter was an even trade for the oppressive summer. And to this day I still attempt to persuade Liz that trading lobster for catfish was a good trade. She's having none of it.

From the horseback-riding ranch we headed north to Jasper, Georgia. Jasper, Ellijay, and surrounding areas are well known for apples and offer some fantastic mountain foliage that, while perhaps not in the major leagues of Vermont, are at least in a Triple-A sort of club. We walked among the orchards picking apples, selecting pumpkins, holding hands, taking in the scenery and just enjoying the outdoors.

Liz thought this was the culmination of her birthday celebration. It was just the beginning.

The plan was to leave Jasper and drive a few hours southeast to Madison, Georgia, where we would stay for two nights at a horseback-riding resort of sorts. We took our time leaving Jasper and meandered over winding roads, taking in the farmland and countryside. In one respect, north Georgia is quite similar to Vermont and New Hampshire. And that is while driving north to south is an easy assignment in all three states via highways, going east to west is only possible via slow-moving roads that snake mountain ranges—the Green Mountains in Vermont, the White Mountains in New Hampshire, and the Blue Ridge mountains in Georgia. In retrospect, I believe that the seeds of our farming life and the life of Nature's Harmony Farm germinated during that drive but we didn't know it at the time. We simply commented to one another how beautiful it all was.

As we arrived at our destination in Madison, everything began to change. This was different. A huge, gorgeous piece of property that could rightly be called a farm—or at least a horse farm. I am not sure what it was that sparked our fire during that stay. Maybe it was staying on a "farm" for the first time that allowed us to visualize living on a farm ourselves. Maybe it was the fact that the horses and the land didn't seem to care what the stock or real estate markets were doing, what the unemployment rate was, what the price of gas was, or if there were a war overseas. They just wanted to know where the water and hay was. Could life be any more elementary, any more perfect than that? Maybe it was the peace and tranquility we felt when riding the horses through the woods. For sure the kindling for our fire was already there in the form of the questions I had already begun asking myself about how we were spending our lives.

During that weekend, Liz and I rode the horses on our own through the woods. If we wanted to stop and look at a majestic tree or a cascading stream, we did. The rules and distractions were few. Apart from the group and on the wooded trails we felt like it was just the two of us on the land. It felt like our land. As we rode there was an opening off the trail, sort of a small clearing where the sun could kiss the ground and entice an array of grasses and flora to reach forth with praise. Liz and I stopped riding for a few minutes and sat in the opening and just *existed*. The profound contentment was obvious on Liz's face when she whispered, "I could really get used to this!" I think my reply surprised her.

"Me too!"

And with that simple exchange in the midst of nature's beauty our path in life changed. With no further discussion the country breeze took the spark, ignited the kindling and started a roaring fire that continues to this day. We sat and talked and agreed right then and there to change our lives and leave the rat race behind. We had never expressed any dissatisfaction with our lives, or any emptiness that needed filling. We didn't need to.

Just as bends in the riding trail obscure what lies ahead, we didn't know where this new journey would take us. We certainly had no ambition at the time to become farmers but we did feel a deep, intense need to reconnect with the land. We felt the calling and we knew we had to go. Still, what we were discussing was a little crazy. After all, how many of us have taken a vacation, fallen in love with an area and contemplated buying a condo or home there, only to come to our senses once we returned home and worked the numbers? But to actually permanently relocate—that's crazy!

Call us crazy.

Abandoning conventional wisdom about thinking things through, mapping it out and planning our future, we pushed full steam ahead and spent every weekend for the next two months looking at properties. Our criteria were simple enough; at least forty to fifty acres, much of it open but with some hardwoods, and within three hours of Atlanta. That way we could get back for concerts, ball games, and the like. In retrospect, how foolish we were then to think we'd have time for that sort of nonsense. I guess I'd seen Skynyrd for the last time.

We sort of figured we'd trade a little piece of very overpriced real estate in the suburbs for a lot of cheap land in the country and have a few horses. Maybe grow some of our own food. Beyond that we hadn't figured out how we'd earn a living or even pay the property taxes. We weren't sure what we were looking for or where to find it. We just knew that we felt an intense yearning to be part of it, though we weren't quite sure what "it" was.

And so like so many other tales, our Green Acres story is one of love. Mainly love for each other and a deep desire to have a life where we could spend all of our time together and not be in separate jobs, but also our passion for animals and nature. We kidded that if we had a lot of land we could have as many dogs as we wanted. We dreamed that we would find some way to live off the land, spend all our time together and get out of the rat race. Our hearts led us to be together and the land was calling to us.

It was a call we couldn't ignore.

FARM BLOG

In June 2007, several months before we began farming and prior to having any animals on the farm, we began blogging about our transition from the city to the country. The Nature's Harmony Farm blog ran for three years and retired in September 2010. Selected blog posts appear in this book at the end of each chapter, and the full archive of all blog posts can be found at:

www.naturesharmonyfarm.com

I Met the Enemy, and He is Us

by Tim Young

From a Nature's Harmony Farm Blog Post, Sep 1, 2007

Today I visited a farmer who had an old trailer for sale that I'm interested in. I didn't realize he was a farmer, as he doesn't think of himself as such. However, I saw that he had a few of those large chicken houses out back, so I asked him about that. He had three in total, and said he processed something like 115,000 chickens at a time, or about one million per year.

When I got home, I grabbed a satellite image of his place.

If you live in Georgia (or the south), I'm sure you've seen a ton of these places. Actually, doesn't look much like what I think of when I think of a farm, but make no mistake, there's lots of food being grown there.

We were interested in his old cotton trailers to make our first egg mobiles. I told him we were going to frame them off and put nest boxes in for layers. He smiled but didn't seem too sure what we were talking about. I asked him how long the chickens took to reach market weight and he said six weeks.

Wow! We've got it down to six weeks now from birth to bag. What he said next surprised me.

"I really like them chickens," he said. "You give 'em that feed and they grow so fast...they'll grow right in front of you."

"I hear they grow so fast they can't even stand up," I said.

"Yep, and that's just the way I like it," was his amiable reply. "They just sit there."

"Probably because they can't get any exercise, all crammed up like that," I suggested.

"I suppose."

And this is when I realized who the enemy was. It's certainly not this farmer. He was a nice man who genuinely seemed to like his job and the chickens. I didn't sense any cruelty in him, or any awareness of cruelty. No, he was just making a living by supplying what the market—his customers—asked for. Cheap, fast, food.

His customers are, of course, all of us. We who go to supermarkets or restaurants, grab what's on sale without asking, knowing or, worst of all, wanting to know where our meat came from, how it was treated or what it was fed. As long as that continues, feedlots, broiler houses, pigs in confinement and battery cages will continue.

CHAPTER 2

Going to the Country

One of the first rural expressions we learned was "the back forty," which is meant to suggest that many rural citizens have a back forty acres that goes unused. In our case, we found a former farmer who had a back seventy-two. His name was George and he lived in a comfortable home with his wife Jane in Elberton, Georgia. They had lived the whole of their lives in Elberton within a half-mile of where both their parents lived the whole of theirs.

Neither Liz nor I had ever even heard of Elberton. Liz being as they call in these parts a "damn Yankee," had an excuse. As for me, I was born in Macon, Georgia. I had moved around Georgia and Florida quite frequently as a child but came to think of the mountains of northeast Georgia in general and the town of Clayton in particular as my home. All my relatives on my mother's side were from Clayton, a picturesque, mountainous, rural destination that has been home to a handful of motion pictures. Most notable was the movie *Deliverance,* in which my great uncle Earl starred in the classic gas station scene when dueling banjos was played. While pumping gas, Earl spoke briefly with Burt Reynolds before busting out clogging as the banjo and guitar picked their epic duel. Yes, I have some serious hillbilly in me, and may have failed to fully disclose all of this to Liz until the marriage was legit.

In any event, Liz can be excused for not knowing anything about where Elberton was. Here I was, having spent half my life in Georgia with Elberton located essentially equidistant between Clayton and Macon, and I had never heard of the place. But it made no difference. It was open land, affordable and just over two hours from Atlanta, so all our criteria were met. We had come across the property by way of a web search of rural properties in Georgia. Naturally, a realtor had to show us the property and she was quick to introduce us to George, who informed us that the property had been on the market for over a year with no takers. Evidently there weren't too many people keen on buying a "back forty" in the middle of nowhere with no prospects of work. Now two city suckers—I mean slickers—had come along.

Like all good realtors this one quickly tapped into what we were looking for. She pointed out the flowing stream that divided the property, while overlooking the fact that there was no way to cross it. "No problem," she said confidently, "you can just put a culvert in the creek." I nodded and made a mental note to look up the word "culvert" when I got home. Similarly, every time we called her to arrange a visit to the property she reported that she had "just seen" a bobcat or some deer on the property although we always somehow just missed these sightings. Maybe she had seen them, maybe not. Either way she was correct that this was what we wanted to hear about and hopefully see.

17

The land was simply serving as a rear protuberance to George's property, something there but not being used, perhaps like an appendix. It was overgrown with weeds up to eight feet tall, had no outbuildings and had no driveway or access.

That isn't what I saw. I visualized beautiful, open pastures, ponds, animals, majestic trees and nature as it should be, or could be. I painted this picture for Liz who loved the story, but pointed out that the pastures were full of broomsedge, pigweed, horse nettle, rocks, thistle, and dog fennel instead of grasses. Actually, she just pointed at all of those "weeds," as we didn't know the names of any of them. Still, I saw not what was there but what was possible, since I have a habit (bad or good, depending on one's perspective) of seeing what I want to see. This trait is shared by many entrepreneurial-type people who see the world as they would like it and then embark to create it, allowing nothing to deter them. And so, this land became my canvas.

George, now in his mid-sixties, had lived on this piece of land for most of his life. For over twenty years he operated a commercial dairy on the land, tending mainly to a herd of up to a hundred Holstein cows, although he had abandoned the dairy business in 1997 and replaced it with a granite cutting business. Only two hundred feet away from the old dairy barn is a large cement slab foundation supporting two huge diamond-tip granite saws that are suspended from an iron railing.

Elberton's self-proclaimed moniker is "The Granite Capital of the World," so it likely made sense to George that the prospects associated with cutting granite would be more attractive than milking cows. Watching the saws rhythmically and automatically cut through huge stones, it occurred to me that the work was probably easier too. Having not been raised on farms I don't think that neither Liz nor I could really appreciate the amount of work that George and Jane had to do, every day of the year, rain or shine, for over twenty years.

As a dairyman, George's day began by going out in the 5:00 a.m. darkness, rounding up a hunded cows that were spread throughout pastures, and driving them back to the milking parlor half a mile away for milking. Jane rose with George and made coffee that he had no time to drink. Later in the morning he may have been able to wolf down the ham biscuit she wrapped for him so he shoved it in his pocket.

The cows' journey would take them up and down gentle hills, traversing woods, open fields and right through the middle of Sally's Creek before, finally, arriving at the dairy barn. The cows liked the coolness of the creek and in the heat of the summer would linger there until George motivated them to forge ahead. Once at the milking barn the cows congregated on a slanted cement slab under a shed near the entrance. The slant was necessary so that the manure could be washed to the rear of the shed where it would drain into a four-inch pipe that flowed to a manure lagoon.

The cows were accustomed to the loud hum of the vacuum system, which despite the thunderous drone comforted them and told them it was time to be milked. In his new dual-six milking parlor, George would be in the pit readying the pulsation system and inflations while the cows jostled for position at the doors. Clarence, one of George's trusted helpers, would go out and push twelve cows in at a time, six on each side of the pit. With the adroit hands of a hibachi chef George pulled down the inflations and affixed them to each teat, going down the line and getting the milk flowing from all six cows in less than sixty seconds. After accomplishing this George turned to the other side of the pit where six cows were patiently awaiting the same treatment. The cows all knew the drill and didn't mind the wait as a wonderfully delicious portion of dairy ration magically presented itself to each of them from a tube that disappeared into the ceiling. Had any of the cows chose to look up to the ceiling and ponder the scenario, which none did, they may have accurately deduced that the hose went through the ceiling and out to the front of the dairy where it was married to a large feed bin. George felt this feed was necessary to maximize milk production, as all dairymen did. George was paid based on milk volume and butterfat content and the battle to balance the income from the milk with the cost of the dairy feed was a perpetual one for George, and one in which he had precisely zero control over either variable. He was paid whatever the current milk price was and likewise he paid what the feed cost. Negotiation on either point was futile.

George was no doubt very proud of the new milking parlor, 1,500-gallon milk tank and 5,000-gallon underground reservoir, which pumped cool water up to misting hoses that would comfort the cows while waiting under the shed in the summer heat. Years later, George would wonder if he ever really owned that dairy, or if the bank had owned it all along. He would use the money he had gained from selling his "back forty" to keep the bank at bay and hope the granite business would treat him more kindly.

When milking was over for the morning the cows would mosey back across the creek to the pastures where they would graze, lounge and chew cud until late afternoon when the process would repeat itself, as it would every day of every year. And so for the cows, the morning's work was over. For George it had just begun. Cows that were sick or had mastitis would have to be attended to. Mastitis would be bad news for George, as it would result in losses in milk production, milk quality and, as a result, income. The cow would still eat so feed costs would remain unchanged but an additional expense in the form a vet visit diminished his income even further. If the vet pre-scribed antibiotics, which was likely, the milk from the mastitic cow could not be sold until there was no trace of drug residues in the cow's system.

Mastitis is caused by any number of bacteria that invade the open teat, hence the need to dip each cow's teat before and after milking to protect the opening. It shows itself visually as an inflammation of the udder tissue and can be fatal. Often it is detected as flakes or clots in the milk, particularly the first part of the milk, which is why George stripped milk from each cow's teat to check prior to milking. It also shows itself to the Department of Agriculture on the milk sample reports in the form of increased somatic cell counts. Beyond an approved somatic cell count threshold milk from mastitic cows can pose a health risk.

Cleaning the stainless steel milking lines and rubber infla-tions after each milking took time and cost George money in chemicals. The same two-inch stainless steel pipes that trans-ported the milk from the cow through the rubber inflations to the bulk milk tank now had to be cleaned. George loaded the cleaning agents and pressed the button triggering the automatic cleaning system, before stepping outside, pulling the biscuit out of his pocket and surveying the hard, dusty ground around him. On a hot July morning there would have been no rain in weeks, causing him to fret about the pastures and calculate how much his feed bill would increase since he had run out of forage. Once his momentary break was over he would then have to hose off manure deposits from one hundred cows on the sheltered cement floor where the cows awaited milking. As he finished, Jane walked his way, which told him that it was time to bottle-feed and tend to all the calves.

Many people don't realize that in order to get milk each cow must be bred repeatedly so that they'll produce milk for their calves. It is this milk that is intercepted instead by the farmer. It seems obvious but the fact that most people don't know this, or at least have never thought of it is illustrative of how far removed we all are from the origin of our food. Milk comes from a jug and the jug comes from the store; enough said.

Cows that didn't breed back on schedule were considered to be "open" and were of no use to the dairy. They made a brief stop at the sale barn before ending up at a fast-food restaurant. Breeding of the cows on almost every dairy didn't happen the way nature intended. That is to say there is no male, or bull, running with cows and, umm, servicing them. That's too old-fashioned. Rather, dairies use frozen semen that may come from anywhere in the world and is stored locally in liquid nitrogen tanks. Each farmer selects the semen from, literally I suppose, a seed catalog, and they select based on the characteristics they hope to breed for. Some bulls are known to "throw" smaller calves. Some are known to produce cows with higher, more uniformed teats that are perfect for automated milking systems. Nowadays, farmers can endeavor to design their herd with the fervor of Versace or Ralph Lauren and hope to increase milking output and butterfat content just enough so they can "make it" and pay the bank. For a dairyman there are no dreams of retiring to a Caribbean island.

In most dairies, after the calf nurses the first time and gets the immunity and antibody benefits of the mother's colostrum, or first milking, it is removed from its mother and bottle-fed a milk replacer. So if George were milking one hundred cows, he and Jane were likely bottle-feeding thirty to fifty calves at a time. It would have been one hundred calves at a time except that George's dairy, like most, bred continually so that the calves were born throughout the year, which allowed for continual milking. The bottle-feeding regimen included mixing up a powdered milk replacer (using real milk would have been too valuable), filling quart jars, screwing on the lid and nipple, and hand-feeding each calf. Depending on the age of the calf, this was done three to four times per day before washing the jars between feedings.

After clean-up from the milking was finished in late morning there may have been time for a quick lunch or errands. More likely, though, a heat was detected on one or more cows and they required artificial insemination quickly. Perhaps a repair was needed, or hay to be cut and stacked or seed to be sown in the pastures for summer or winter grazing. Then it was back to the parlor to repeat for the evening milking.

Sleep would have come easy that night for George, trumping even the worry about the bank loan and feed costs that danced through his head after he wearily climbed into bed. This process repeated itself every day, year in and year out. Vacations were out of the question, as it was rather difficult to find someone to come in and milk George's hundred cows for him twice a day. The adage is true—farming is a hard life.

Without even discussing it I figured I understood why George opted to leave the cows behind. For ten years now the land that used to feed so many cows lay fallow, becoming a case study for how nature can and will reclaim pasture land. When we visited the property for the first time we stood at George's house on the paved road and he pointed back to the land. A small creek named Sally's creek ran across the property and, according to George, you were required to ford the creek to get back to "our" land. I nodded with a confidence that conveyed I knew precisely what fording the creek meant. I did not.

Confidence being my forte, Liz and I went full speed ahead in our bright shiny F-150, bumping through pasture gullies that reminded me of skiing moguls in Vermont. Driving where there was no road, we were jostled nearly out of our seats as we slowly bounced down the hill. I suspect that silently we each seriously questioned what we were doing. We so wanted to live in the country, yet at this moment I am certain that we each became aware of how far we were out of our element. We were used to paved roads, covenant committees, in-ground sprinkler systems and manicured lawns. Here we were bouncing over who knows what going to who knows where. Why were we doing this again? Was our enthusiasm for moving to the country waning now that we confronted the make-or-break reality of the decision? Had we really thought this thing through?

No, we had not. Nevertheless we forged ahead. Time would tell if that would be a choice we would regret.

We came down to a trodden earthen ramp that led to the creek and noticed a muddy, grassy slope going up the other side. "I guess we're supposed to drive through," I said. Liz tightened her seat belt and employed her customary reflex of grabbing the armrest, as if that would help her. For a moment we just sat in the truck, staring ahead at the stream, as if trying to muster courage. Somehow, crossing the stream seemed to be more than a minor physical obstacle. It seemed to represent a metaphoric hurdle to what was happening in our lives. In a very real way, the stream divided dependent urban life from independent rural life and if we crossed it we might not turn back.

And so we did, and so we didn't.

Shifting into four-wheel drive we made haste into the creek where, for no apparent reason, I momentarily paused. Parked in the middle of the creek I looked first left then right at the trickle of water that seemed to divide our urban existence from an agrarian one. Taking Liz's hand, I charged up the other side where we took pride in the enormity of our accomplishment.

Liz breathed a sigh of relief that she had survived the ordeal.

Facing up a slope our eyes fixed on a thick line of trees and brush that crossed our path, much like a windbreak. A closer examination of the windbreak revealed strands of barbed wire weaving in and out of trees, entering the ground here and exiting there, looking to us like a medieval torture device. Like many farmers, George had long ago woven a series of barbed wire fence lines throughout the property. Over time countless wild birds frequented George's farm, rested on these fence lines, and gratuitously dropped pre-fertilized seeds that would sprout into large oak, sycamore, hackberry, elm, locust, and countless other trees. The results of the birds' efforts were now visible in this voluntary windbreak of trees that, ironically, provided nesting spots for future generations of birds. Even we city slickers could tell where the fences had been and it would be we city slickers who would have to clean this mess up.

Behind the line of trees were wide-open fields of waist-high brown stuff. I figured it might be tumbleweed or something that I had heard of in a western movie. Later I learned it was broomsedge, a weedy plant that is a sure indicator of highly acidic soil. Virtually no trees claimed residence in the pastures, a fact that made it convenient for George to harvest hay. It also made it difficult for animals to find shade, not to mention robbing us of beauty that would have been otherwise granted by a lone, majestic tree.

After we forded the creek I put the truck into gear and started up the slope. Entering the weedy unknown, the weeds rose higher than the sides of the truck, similar to being in a snow bank. I would later learn that broomsedge doesn't grow this high. Dog fennel, pigweed, jimson and yellow crown-beard do however, and we were driving through heaps of it. Frequently while driving through the weeds there would be a loud "thump" and the truck would heave, so I crept gingerly. After being heaved a few times I got out to discover the cause. Rocks. Huge rocks! Granite capital indeed!

Clearly the land didn't look perfect and was more like your pasture fixer-upper. But it felt right and George seemed nice, so we fell in love with this piece of land where we would, we hoped, live out our years and, if we were lucky, have children who would live out theirs. And so it was that in January 2007, just three months after our horseback riding adventure, we found ourselves with seventy-two acres in the middle of nowhere where we knew no one, and only then realizing that maybe we hadn't completely thought this through. Would we be able to handle the emotional transition from a world of surplus and convenience to a relatively isolated existence? Could we give up vacations, spontaneity, security and a social life?

It was too late then as the time had come to find the answer to each of these questions for ourselves. Having nursed at the teats of convenience too long, it was time for us to be weaned.

ℓℓ

Elberton, Georgia is *not* the place to go if you're looking for good sushi. Or any sushi! We *loved* sushi so this presented a real problem for us. Before moving to our greener pastures we routinely enjoyed sushi twice a week. We would sit at the bar, watching the sushi chef work miracles and speaking with the owner. Like the character Norm from Cheers we were regulars.

Sushi wasn't all I was hooked on.

If faced with the daunting task of brewing a pot of coffee I may instead have been lured by a coffee shop not too far away. This decision was easily rationalized by the exotic array of coffee drinks from which I could choose that, as far as I was concerned, were far beyond my reach as a home barista.

I won't lie about it. Letting go of our addiction to sushi was difficult for both Liz and me. We still long for sushi and it's our indulgence of choice today when we deliver to customers in urban areas. If I find myself hoping someone will whip up a "venti latte" for me today the closest thing around these parts is at McDonalds, unless I want to drive an hour to the college town of Athens. In these parts the preferred coffee is Maxwell House, as it has always been.

OK, so there's no sushi and no Starbucks. Who needs it, I ask myself, as I go out to work on one of our first farm projects. Today my plan is to build an eggmobile out of an old cotton wagon that I bought locally. An eggmobile is a fitting name given to a mobile hen house that houses several hundred hens. It is pulled around the pasture so that it is situated two or three days behind where the cows have been. This way the hens can eat grass and scratch through cow pies looking for juicy grubs to eat. For this project I'll need some lumber and supplies to frame the sides and roof so I'll just run to Home… no wait, there's no do-it-yourself home center within an hour's drive. I can't take that for granted anymore. I'll have to plan my trips carefully or I'll spend a fortune in time and fuel.

Elberton does of course have a Wal-Mart. Beyond that there is an astonishing number of fast-food joints, two Mexican restaurants, several liquor stores, countless churches and about a half-dozen auto parts stores. The concentration of liquor stores strikes me as being at odds with the number of churches, something I contemplate as I offer thanks—for the liquor stores.

While setting up the farm before we moved to Elberton we made a point to try as many of the local dining establishments as we could during our visits. On a side street in town we were pleasantly surprised to find an Italian restaurant with a bar, so Liz and I had dinner there one night. Having been spoiled by the fantastically authentic Italian food in Boston's North End and Providence's Federal Hill we tempered our expectations just a bit, and we were right to expect just a little less. Whereas we had once dined to the intoxicating smell of house-made sauces and fresh baked cannoli, this Italian restaurant employed the novel approach of using pasta sauce from a jar. I wasn't able to tell if it was Ragu or another brand but it fairly complemented the pasta, which emerged from a blue and white box.

Since we intended Elberton to be our home for the rest of our lives, prior to moving there we wanted to learn as much as we could about it. Subscribing to the local newspaper seemed a logical way to accomplish this and so we did. Small-town newspapers focus on very different types of local stories than do the large metropolitan newspapers and we found ourselves reading the detailed police report logs more than any other section. Four of the stories we read amused us greatly.

According to the paper one person reported that a pile of dirt was stolen from her driveway but that it was later returned to a different spot. She didn't actually see the dirt being taken, it was just now in a different location from what she recalled. Another report detailed a complaint about a neighbor who was mowing the grass. Nothing strange about that, except he was reportedly wearing only his underwear. A third story transcended the police report section and earned the headline "Man charged with beating brother with frying pan." Naturally this piqued my interest. According to the report one of the brothers, John, was eating in the kitchen when his brother began spraying bug spray in the kitchen to kill maggots. An argument ensued and John walked outside to put gas in the lawnmower so he could leave. For some reason the brother came out, put John in a headlock and started hitting him in the head with a frying pan. John responded by biting his brother in the side. Yikes!

Finally, the crème de la crème. It was reported that a thief, completely nude, broke into a house on a street quite close to where our property is located. A subsequent search of the house showed nothing taken save a stash of candy bars from the kitchen cupboard. The candy bars were later found in the clothes dryer. Yep, the birthday suit thief had broken in and relocated the candy bars from point A to point B, but took nothing. Just guessing here but drugs may have played a role.

Well, we weren't in Kansas anymore.

Most of the 4,500 citizens of Elbert County work in the granite industry in one way or another. Indeed, approximately forty percent of the town's non-farm wage earners owe their employment in some measure to the granite quarries, plants, service firms, or saws like the one George operates.[1]

Just over half of the people in Elberton are listed as white, non-Hispanic, with approximately forty percent recorded as black, resulting in a relatively equal divide. During one of our early conversations George relayed a story to us concerning the town's ambulances. Evidently several years prior George drove one of the county's ambulances. Belonging to the white non-Hispanic group, George would on occasion be called to a scene where a black person was in need of assistance. If that were the case the protocol was clearly established and George simply called one of the "black" ambulances. They would come and take care of "their kind" and return the favor should they be inadvertently summoned to help a white person. Liz is unfailingly polite but I could see behind the curtain of her smile that she was aghast. Being raised in Massachusetts, she was unfamiliar with this kind of talk. I, on the other hand, did remember from my Georgia child-hood the bias of racial divide. The generation before me had lived through these issues much more dramatically in Georgia than the generation before Liz had in Massachusetts. Still this startled me as well.

The thing is, George didn't mean anything derogatory about it. This was just how things were back then.

C'est la vie.

Clearly we were in a different environment and we were the ones who would have to adapt. Fortunately the ambulance story would soon fade into my memory once I met Randy.

Randy lived up the road from us and was the first acquaintance I made after I met George. Short, skinny, always greasy, and never without his floppy hat, Randy had a reputation of being able to fix anything. His yard was something that I used to consider a junk heap with dozens of machines in various stages of repair, or disrepair, depending on one's point of view. When we bought the land from George we asked if we could have the weeds mowed so we could get a better view. In the country this is referred to as "bush hogging," which owes its name to the mower pulled by the tractor. Unlike a finish or grass mower, a bush hog is designed to cut through heavy weeds and brush, in some cases up to a few inches in diameter. That's what we needed for our woody fields.

When Liz and I came back for a trip to see the property, Randy had cleared it for us without us asking, and he declined to take payment. Maybe we weren't insistent enough—upon reflection, I don't know. I suspect we should have paid anyway but I remember not knowing the protocol in this bizarre new world. Nevertheless, Randy made his way on to my speed dial quickly and became one of my favorite people anywhere. I've known people with far more education, experience, money and influence (oh, and ego too) than Randy will ever have but none of them can do the "real" things that Randy does.

Still, despite being someone I'm fond of, I won't mince words: Randy is what many people refer to as a redneck. His beliefs, due in part to his upbringing, make him sometimes seem prejudice against people who are different from him. Then again he's not the only person like that, now is he?

According to George, because Randy had moved to Elberton only twenty years ago, he was still considered an outsider. Clearly, in our lifetimes there was no hope for us to join the inner circle.

Randy spoke softly and in a dialect that was remarkably difficult to understand. I always had to ask him to repeat himself and he always politely obliged. If I spoke to him on the phone I'd ask him multiple times to repeat himself. Even as a Georgian this was a language with which I wasn't familiar.

During our first year on the farm both George and Randy made a habit of driving over to see us whenever they got the notion. Of course Liz and I would always be in the midst of working feverishly trying to set up the farm. No matter; the expectation in these parts is that you stop what you're doing and sit for a spell. A spell was always at least an hour.

I wasn't blessed with an abundance of patience so it was frustrating for me to be pulled off my work, and, regrettably, it probably showed. Today, George and Randy don't come around as often, partly because they're busy on their own and partly, I suspect, because they likely figure we no longer need looking after. Now like the rebellious teenager who as an adult wishes for one more home-cooked meal like the ones he used to complain about, I sometimes look down the driveway and wish they would drive back. I gladly stop whatever I am doing to visit with them anytime they do.

Randy tended to come over more frequently than George. Even though he was a large equipment mechanic in the granite industry, he also kept some cows and I think he was interested in the wacky kind of farming we were telling him about. Having grown up in north Georgia I had known a lot of good, hardworking country folk like Randy. To Liz however, Randy was as alien as Chewbacca and she was thrilled to meet a real-life, honest to goodness, down-south country bumpkin! Keenly aware of how different she was from Randy, all Liz could ponder was what did Randy think of her and was she coming off like a fancy city slicker, something she wanted to avoid. Cleverly she would try to direct the conversation and let him talk; only to find out he generally had nothing to say. So she'd probe deeper and ask insightful questions about stuff he knew so that he could have the upper hand in the conversation.

"How do you know when the cows are about to have a baby?" Liz would ask. This question was weighing heavily on

Liz's mind as we were about to take possession of our new cows, and she was panicking about all that she did not know.

"You'll see 'em spring up," Randy replied with a certain rural nonchalance.

"Spring up—what does that mean?" Liz probed.

"They'll bag up," was Randy's reply, drawn out longer than I thought possible for a three-word response. No matter how many times you asked Randy to repeat or explain himself, his voice always remained calm and soft spoken.

Liz stared perplexed, and there was a long silence. She had no idea what Randy meant by "bag up," but she resisted the temptation to confess this out of fear that it might blow her cover.

"Uh...could you describe what it might look like when a cow bags up?" Liz pressed.

With a sly grin, Randy held his arms around his chest and said, "They'll look like Dolly Parton on steroids!" No further detail was offered.

Liz thought about it. "Oh," Liz said, "you mean the bag is the udder and it gets filled with milk because—I get it—she's gonna have a baby. Right?"

Now Randy looked perplexed.

Right from the start we became very fond of Randy and I found myself having many long conversations with him, something I continue to do today. Given our very different backgrounds there are many points on which we disagree but I always choose to leave it at that and focus on common ground. When he came by he would talk I would listen and I didn't judge. I hoped he wouldn't either. He is who he is as I am who I am. We have different backgrounds, different life experiences and, as a result, different values and perspectives. We can see the world differently and still be friends, and we are.

Life is very different out here. Weaning for us was more than getting used to living without the conveniences we had once enjoyed. It was also about adapting to an alien environment and facing the cold reality that now it was *we* who were the aliens. Urban living is all about convenience. Whatever you need there is a store or solution reasonably close by, easily identifiable by an endless line of traffic in low-speed pursuit. The perceived benefit of this reality is of course subjective. We moved in part due to the box stores that were beginning to encircle us, slowly moving in for the kill on our wallet. Within just a few miles of where we formerly lived was every conceivable type of restaurant, organic grocery store, specialty and large-scale retail, pet grooming, lumber and landscaping centers, malls, concert arenas, professional sports teams, museums, theaters, nightclubs, you name it. We felt drawn to many of these places, I think, simply because they were there.

Some of the conveniences were considered necessities, for if there were an emergency many fine hospitals and doctors were close to where we formerly lived, including many top specialists. The fact that specialists were now so far away was particularly relevant for us at the time. Quite often Randy would bring his two children by when we were cleaning up the pastures, and we always loved watching Mary Beth and Slayter run and play in the pastures while we worked. Mary Beth was seven and Slayter was five, both perfect ages to explore our woods and creeks yet old enough to help around the farm. It was wonderful having children on the farm—only we didn't have any of our own.

When we bought the land Liz and I had been trying for two years to conceive a child with no luck and, perhaps most frustrating of all, with no doctor able to explain why. Supposedly we were both quite capable. Nowadays, during farm tours the most common question we are asked by far is if we have children. I am not sure how Liz feels when this question is asked. For sure we both have emotions underneath the surface that range from anger to love to embarrassment. We love the idea of having children and we're angry that the answer is "no," but perhaps we're embarrassed that we don't have the "right" answer—the answer that everyone expects and the answer we so long for. People know or at least expect that as farmers we're supposed to have children. That's part of the farm dream, having children to grow up and take over the farm, something we dreamt about as we added bedrooms and space to the large new house we built. So having children and raising them in the country was a very real part of our farm dream and we were becoming desperate enough when we bought the land to consider seeking the sorcery of fertility specialists. These specialists would be in Atlanta, however, and would be anything but convenient.

We pondered the impact this distance would have on our plans but the long distance combined with our ongoing lack of success made us feel as though we were being conspired against. By this point in our lives the emotional stress of being childless was becoming more than either of us could bear to deal with, evidenced by the fact that we increasingly didn't talk about it, choosing instead to gingerly sidestep the issue. Like clockwork, once a month we received very heartbreaking news until one day, for me, the reports ceased coming at all. As countless other couples know it just hurts too much to talk about. When you're trying so hard and when you're so hopeful, it becomes all you can think about.

In the end, without explanation or apology, you are simply denied.

Still we would continue to try without either confessing as much, and cling to a thread of hope that our wish for a family could be granted.

Fortunately Elberton did have a small hospital that instilled a sense of security should we require emergency care, but specialists, fertility or otherwise, were more of the agrarian type. In the 1980s movie *Baby Boom*, Diane Keaton, having just moved to rural Vermont, fainted and found herself being attended by a doctor. As she regained consciousness and groggily revealed the innermost secrets of her love life to the doctor she became shocked to see animals around her, only then realizing that the doctor was a veterinarian. Likewise in rural areas such as ours top medical specialists are those who can pull a calf or artificially inseminate a cow. This may prove to be of little comfort to those humans in need of medical attention. Upon realization of this fact Liz became uncomfortable early on in our farm life as she faced the double whammy of on one hand having fewer medical resources and on the other an onslaught of potential attackers in the form of spiders, ticks, chiggers and snakes.

We bought the property in the middle of winter, so until the weather warmed up, Liz wasn't afforded an opportunity to appreciate the creepy, crawly wonders with which she would now share a habitat.

On a warm day in spring Liz began scratching her legs after picking up rocks in the pasture.

"I have a rash or something," Liz said in a controlled pre-panic.

It's possible that I could walk around with a broken arm dangling by my side without noticing, but Liz can detect an embryonic hive on her face two days before it appears. With doom in her voice she'll say to me, "Do you see a hive here?" I'll touch, peer and get out my magnifying glass, but feel nothing, see nothing. Two days later it's there and I am admonished for not having been able to detect it.

Now Liz has the itchies. "What is this?" she exclaims.

"Just chiggers," I reply, thinking nothing about it. Having been raised in Georgia, I don't think there's anyone here that not only doesn't know what a chigger is and accepts these co-inhabitants as a simple reality of life. We share the same habitat.

"What's a chigger? Are you making that up?"

This hadn't occurred to me. Liz didn't know what a chigger was! Oh boy, would she be finding out! How should I break this to her? Chiggers are ferocious! Once the springtime temperature stops getting too cold at night, chiggers emerge, especially in grass, and boy did we have a lot of tall grass! They have a habit of making you itch, and in all the wrong places. You can't see chiggers with the naked eye but you'll see evidence of their visit. Their bites near hair follicles leave the victim covered with red, painfully itchy blotches that suggest a sudden, inexplicable rash. The chiggers escaped Liz's visual notice but their attack didn't.

"A chigger is a little bug that bites you in the grass," I answered. I didn't know anything scientific like that they are the larvae of harvest mites or anything fancy like that. As a child I was just told that they were chiggers and accepted that.

Of course, Liz's worst fears set in as she set out on a quest to learn what diseases the chiggers might be carrying. Randy threw gas on the fire by informing Liz that they were burrowing into her skin as most people here are told, and her concern escalated to a heightened level. For the record it isn't true that chiggers burrow into your skin but Randy was having none of that. George was simply amused by the whole thing.

"Could be fire ants," George offered, pronouncing it like "far ants." This did not assuage Liz's concern.

"Fire ants—what are *those*?" Liz asked intently.

"Oh, you'll find out soon enough," George chuckled.

Fire ants are nasty and the mention of them momentarily distracted Liz from chiggers. Aggressive, stinging and ubiquitous in the south, fire ants attack before you know it. Without even thinking, the victim of the fire ant attack will start scratching before quickly becoming intensely motivated to scratch fiercely all over. Looking down, panic overwhelms them as they spot the mound of thousands of angry fire ants on which they're standing. Usually it's ankles and legs that are most affected and if you live in their presence, you'll spend the better part of the year with visible bumps and a rash in those areas. Everyone has them. As we walked our new pastures I pointed out for Liz the countless fire ant mounds that shared our property.

Fortunately, on our farm today they are few and far between, a debt we owe to our free-ranging feathered friends.

To Liz the onslaught of all of this predator overload data gave the surreal impression of being immersed in a science fiction novel. First chiggers, now fire ants, what other alien life forms would she now have to battle? That's when she discovered our population of ticks.

Ticks were something that Liz was very well aware of in Massachusetts. As a border state to Connecticut, where the dreaded Lyme disease originated, Massachusetts residents are keenly aware of the bacterial infection caused by deer ticks. Early stages of Lyme disease include rash and flu-like symptoms. So how did Liz know that I was right and her rash was from chigger bites and not a fierce Lyme-disease-carrying tick?

When a choice is presented to believe either me, or a much worse scenario, Liz never opts to believe me.

In the end Liz accepted ticks, snakes, ants, spiders and chiggers as our neighbors, but a larger obstacle loomed that nearly dashed our farm dreams before they even began.

In early 2007, shortly after having acquired the property, we visited the vacant farm. The land looked remarkably different with signs of green everywhere and grasses knee-high. Liz and I strolled out into the waist-high fescue.

"Achoo!"

"Bless you," I said, in response to Liz's sneeze.

I smiled and looked over to her, only then noticing that she was standing dead still in the pasture with her hand clutched alarmingly around her throat. She was having a severe allergic reaction and I didn't know what was happening. Like many people Liz had suffered from seasonal allergies in the past but she thought she had outgrown them. Indeed, they never exposed themselves in our manicured suburban landscape. Our new paradise resembled a natural stadium, with every imaginable tree forming the spectators, enveloping us as participants on a playing field woven with every conceivable grass, weed, forbs, herb and wildflower.

All of this stimulation was too much for Liz's immune system. Her throat became itchy and began to contract, so she couldn't speak and had difficulty breathing. She grabbed my arm and moved very slowly as she signaled that we needed to leave. Quickly we got in the truck and headed toward town, and Liz's condition started to improve almost immediately.

"Oh no!" I thought to myself and said to no one. "What have we done? We can't live out here." Our life in the country was about to end much more abruptly than it began. As Liz was recovering from a panic brought on by allergies, *my* panic was setting in about not only her condition, but what would become of our new property and our life. After another half hour she began to feel fine so we stopped for lunch where I was able to broach the subject of allergies with her.

"Liz, you can't live out here. What should we do?"

"I'll be all right" she replied. "I just need to be careful when the grass is tall and the trees are all in bloom." I was thinking that would be most of the time, but I think we both realized that we were already committed to this journey. We would have to forge ahead, but Liz's experience led us down a path that resulted in our raising bees for local honey to help her with her allergies.

Even though I didn't suffer from allergies, this gave me pause to reflect on what was happening to society as a whole. How have we all arrived at a point where we, human animals, can't even go into a field without being overcome by allergies? Does anyone honestly think this was a problem a thousand years ago? We've created such a perfect manmade world that we, the inhabitants who created it, cannot live outside of it.

❧

I suppose that much of what we experienced were the obvious weaning experiences one would expect when moving to the country, but there are countless others that bordered on the subliminal. In the end we came to view some of the things we lost in moving to the country as additions and not subtractions.

Take, for example, the absence of large box stores. It is true that there is no large home improvement store in Elberton, but a wonderful discovery I made was finding a store called

Southern Farm and Hardware. Owned by two brothers, Rob and Kevin, the store strikes me as something from a time long ago. They carry an assortment of items necessary to live out here including Carhartt clothing, plumbing and electrical supplies, animal feeds and medications, fencing supplies, and a bare minimum assortment of necessary hardware. Closed on Sundays and with a ceiling barely seven feet high, they will never be confused with a large orange box store but—and this is a big "but"—the service there is like from a general store a hundred years ago. Norman Rockwell would be proud!

In the first few years I lived in Elberton I would find myself countless times bringing simple projects to Kevin and Rob and marvel as they would stop what they were doing and take a half hour to help me find the fifty-cent part I needed to make my project work before sending me on my way. In the beginning I compared with amusement this small store to the large stores. Now whenever I find myself in the large stores I may marvel at their diversity, but buy only what I absolutely must, saving every other penny I have for Rob and Kevin with the aim of doing my part to keep these kind of stores alive. I'm no longer a regular at a sushi bar but I am a regular at Southern Farm and Hardware, where the coffee is bad and the people are real reminders of what we all can and should be—honest, hard-working, helpful and committed to one another.

Another benefit of living out here in the country has to do with landscaping. In our urban community all the neighbors had their own form of Olympic competition around lawn care with unspoken awards for the person whose lawn would green up first in the spring. Out here we don't have to mow at all, much less worry about whether to bag or mulch, as the cows and sheep are happy to bag and fertilize.

Before, we lived right next door to people whose names we did not know. Now, we belong to a community where we know others and where we are known. We know where to get help, whom to call and we're eager to help whenever we can. We count our neighbors as friends, share stories of grief and happiness, and walk through life more together and less alone. In the end we have survived our weaning ordeal, and learned to live with only occasional sushi, making our own coffee, limited health care, slow Internet, ticks, chiggers, snakes, allergies, dust, and strange new neighbors. We rarely miss the mothership and the longer we're here the more we're grateful that we're not there, wherever there may be. We actually did what many people talk and dream about and what other people may consider to be crazy. We opted out—out of the industrial food system, out of bumper-to-bumper traffic, out of cubicles, out of hyper-inflated land prices and out of living in artificial communities to which no one really belongs.

We picked up, left the rat race behind and moved to the country, momentarily forgetting that there was one lingering, minor problem we needed to address.

We had no idea how we would make a living out here.

COUNTRY NEIGHBORS
BY TIM YOUNG

From a Nature's Harmony Farm Blog Post, March 11, 2008

When you look to move to the country, you typically find a real estate agent or start searching online for land that has the physical characteristics you desire. Acreage, pasture or woods, ponds, proximity to desired locations and similar criteria are common on the list. Then you find your property, make your offer and before you know it you're living in the country.

What's missing from this list? Probably the single most important criterion: the neighbors. Surprisingly, you rarely get to really know who are your neighbors before you move in. What are they like, and will you get along? Some people make the mistake of thinking if they move to a lot of land then the neighbors won't matter. Those people are missing the point, I think, and missing out one of the best parts of the country. We have seventy-two acres and could easily keep to ourselves if we wanted. But we don't want that.

We have two neighbors whom we see almost every day. George is the person we bought the property from. He still has eleven acres in front of us, so we have "the back pasture." George runs a granite sawmill as part of those eleven acres. In years past, he ran a dairy operation on our farm, but stopped that in 1997. George has been "here" his whole life. It's funny—we think that we live in "Elberton," which is a pretty small town. Then we found out we live in "Fortsonia," which is a small area (with a gas station and a nursing home, that's it) south of Elberton. But really, we don't even live there, as George talks about Fortsonia (two miles from us) as a faraway land.

I'm not really sure where we live, but I know that George knows everyone. In forty years, if George is still alive, we'll still be new-comers to him. He's a great neighbor who has lent a hand on many occasions. He drives back, checks on the progress of our house, and salivates over what he calls our cows (steak on a hoof). Then he dreams of getting catfish out of our pond, though he has lost the ambition to fish and instead says he'll bring a net.

George recently gave us a piece of granite and had it polished so we could use it for a farm sign at our entrance. We had the sign engraved, and then George donated the base to set it in. Then he, one of his workers and his nephew came over with their crane truck and set it for us. The price? No charge. I never get to pay. Coming from more populous areas, this is a hard adjustment. But I told George that I guess I'd owe him some beef for all the favors. He commented that he figured we were already on the second cow now!

And then, there is Randy. Randy lives in the next house, and even though he's been here for over twenty years or so, he's really from Oglethorpe County (next county over) so he's kind of an outsider. Randy is a real country boy, always sporting a floppy hat, thin as a rail and doesn't own anything that isn't broken or pasted together. But Randy is one of the best people I've ever met. First of all, he can flat out fix anything mechanical. You know the type; always tinkering and can make anything work. That's Randy. Secondly, Randy is very generous with his time and is always willing to lend a hand. And that's good news for me! In the past nine months, I've had to learn all kinds of things I've never done before, and between Randy and George, they know them all. Driving tractors, dealing with faulty PTO shafts, three-point hitches and tractor implements, adding electrical circuits, running irrigation line, plowing, bush hogging, fencing—you name it. I was more comfortable making high-level executive presentations or perhaps working on technology contraptions. Now I'm in a different world, a world in which I'm not so smart and in need of an education and a helping hand.

I still have a lot courage and confidence though, so Randy and George are always watching to make sure I don't hurt myself too badly. I can't tell you how many times Randy has bailed me out. Last week when Liz and I were at the Georgia Organics conference and gone for three days, Randy was there every day to move our cows. That may sound easy, but you have to move the water and just check on things. Plus both George and Randy have a great sense of humor, and anyone who knows Liz or me knows we love to laugh all the time.

The best home security system in the country is good neighbors. Our driveway is almost three thousand feet long and goes right past George's house. Since it's gravel, Randy can hear anyone going down the driveway as well. There have been many times when George has called us telling us that someone is at our house (normally the builder or a contractor). They really look out for us!

When we looked for our farm, we didn't interview the neighbors. And we wouldn't have known then what a good country neighbor was anyway. But we lucked out. We really appreciate our neighbors, and I hope we get the chance to help them in some way at some point, but it's hard to imagine how we can.

CHAPTER 3

The Accidental Farmers

Having impetuously acted on our urge to move to the country, we found ourselves confronting a serious quandary. In a rural area with high unemployment and below-average demographics, what exactly would we do to make a living for a lifetime? The goals that drove us to move to the country were the same ones we hear expressed today by many people when they visit our farm. We wanted the pastoral beauty of the country, the laid-back lifestyle and the peaceful, easy feeling that we assumed everyone out here enjoyed. We also wanted a place to which we could belong. We had lived in our suburban Atlanta subdivision for three years within feet of our neighbors. Still, we didn't know any of them. Oh, we saw them every now and then at a social event, but perhaps you understand what I mean when I say we didn't *know* them. We wanted to live among people we would know, whom we could count on and who could count on us. That was a hole in our life that needed filling.

We were at an awkward yet opportunistic time where we had just agreed to purchase the property, but had no immediate plans to move there and weren't sure what to do with it. Indeed, there was no place to live on the property. Stuck in suburbia with dreams of finding a way to make a living in the country but with no home yet in the country in which to live, we began reading voraciously. Not surprisingly the first books we read had to do with horses. I had given Liz some for Christmas since we had such a great time horseback riding three months earlier and having horses seemed a natural next step. We would thumb through books in search of anything that would connect us to our new life. Sipping coffee in a local bookstore we became fascinated with the idea of homesteading and producing as much food for ourselves as we could. This led us to read books on gardening, growing mushrooms, constructing farm buildings and the like. Eventually we discussed having farm animals such as a pig, and this led us to reading books about livestock. It was if we had just walked through the looking glass into a new world where everything was new to us. We soaked up everything we read.

As our knowledge grew so too did our awareness, both about the opportunities before us as well as the problems faced by our society at large. We found ourselves being drawn to provocative and resourceful books that gave us more serious matters to contemplate. Those books included:

- *The Omnivore's Dilemma: A Natural History of Four Meals*, by Michael Pollan

- *Slaughterhouse: The Shocking Story of Greed, Neglect, and Inhumane Treatment Inside the U.S. Meat Industry*, by Gail Eisnitz

- *The Contrary Farmer* by Gene Logsdon

- *You Can Farm!* by Joel Salatin
- *Silent Spring* by Rachel Carson
- *The Soil and Health* by Sir Albert Howard

Since you're reading this book you may already be familiar with one or more of the ones I mentioned above. Pollan's *The Omnivore's Dilemma* was an instant classic and opened many people's eyes, including ours, to how our food is produced, how it's grown and (just my interpretation) how consumers have been manipulated. Pollan's investigative work and ability to synthesize pieces of the food chain that are beyond reach for most of us definitely gave me pause and something to consider.

Liz too moved on from the dreamy horse books to something more serious of her own. Since we had been discussing for the first time having farm animals, she picked up a copy of *Slaughterhouse* and read first-hand accounts of what takes place inside America's slaughterhouses. She wasn't able to finish the book and deeply considered a vegan lifestyle. While sitting in our living room one evening she audibly sighed in disgust about the words she absorbing from the pages of *Slaughterhouse*. On that particular night, I was reading *You Can Farm!* by Joel Salatin, whom, coincidentally, I had just read about in *The Omnivore's Dilemma*.

Salatin, a lifelong farmer, wasn't only passionate about his method of farming but was evidently successful living off the five hundred and fifty acres he had inherited in Virginia. In the book he described his views on various farm enterprises with the fervor of a salvation minister while promulgating his scripture of "natural" farming. Much of it sounded beautiful, with the author using quaint, descriptive, emotive phrases such as "the piggy-ness of the pig" or the "chicken-ness of the chicken" to describe how his animals should be able to express themselves. The model of farming he wrote about seemed quaint and brought to mind the images consistent with what we as a society collectively believe that farm life should embrace. Still, there were a number of ideas in the book that struck me as curious. Notably was the author's insistence that there was no place on the farm for pets, such as dogs, or non-contributing assets, such as horses. That wouldn't work for us. Moreover, in order to survive financially it sounded to me like everything had to operate at maximum efficiency, that profit-ability was of utmost importance, and that there was no room for modest luxuries such as a modern house or decent car. My reason in leaving corporate America was in part due to the obsessive focus on efficiency, productivity and quarterly profits, and I wasn't looking to find those pressures in farming. We wanted to live off the land and had no illusions about getting rich doing so. But the real kicker was when the author stated firmly that if you were forty-five or older it was too late for you to get into farming. Shucks! Being almost forty-six at the time, I laughed at this generalization. I still do today.

I contemplated why a farmer couldn't aspire to the same white-collar success that urban professionals such as doctors, lawyers and consultants do. As farmers we wouldn't need to be treated better than other professionals but why couldn't we be treated equally? An investment in land costs at least as much as an investment in education and isn't it just as worthwhile to prevent illnesses through producing "clean" food as it is for a doctor to treat later-stage illnesses?

My attention was taken from my book as Liz slammed *Slaughterhouse* down on the table. With a look of utter repugnance she said, "I can't read any more of this."

I said, "You know, there may be another way."

I shared what I had been reading and suggested for the first time the notion of becoming farmers. She stared at me for a moment and pondered what I had said before replying.

"Do you mean like real farmers? Like, make a *living* from it? Do people still do that?"

Up until our crash course in farming literature, I think we may have thought that there were no farms, or at least there were no people making a living from farming. Our naiveté was shocking but there it was.

"Yes, I think there may be a way that makes sense," I said. "But I don't know."

And I didn't.

Given my background in business it fell to me to think through the economics of this notion, to create spreadsheets in my mind based on assumptions about enterprises with which I had zero experience and knowledge. Liz was interested in the idea because she loves animals, but from the outset she preferred the idea of homesteading with a small number of animals rather than farming on a larger scale for others. It's an ongoing tug-of-war between us that we wage still today.

The idea of homesteading is charming and can dramatically reduce your living expenses while increasing your independence. Still, taxes need to be paid, medical expenses pop up and if you want to save anything you need to generate at least *some* income. I pointed this out to Liz and continued thinking about our path, although we cemented two critical realizations that evening that would shape our future:

We firmly established our utter disgust with factory farming methods; and,

We became completely aware of how completely unaware we were of where our food came from and how it was produced.

Of course we weren't alone in being naïve about the American food production system. It was like Clinton's Don't Ask/Don't Tell policy—the food just kept coming from somewhere and we all kept putting it away. Pollan's writings opened a lot of people's eyes to this issue. What made the realization different for us was that we now had some land and we were looking for something worthwhile we could do to make a living with it. For our own food we became aware that we could go to farmers' markets to get local produce. Farmers' markets were just starting to really take off and there were a number of growers of local vegetables. However, notwithstanding the horrors of *Slaughterhouse*, Liz and I enjoyed eating meat. Where was the humanely raised meat? Pasture-raised or grass-fed meats like those that I had just read about were foreign to us. Indeed, web searches disclosed no local farms that in any way resembled the farm about which Pollan had written so eloquently. Many fruit and vegetable growers at local farmers' markets grow their bounties on small parcels of land, often an acre or less, and while substantial quantities of produce can be produced sustainably on small parcels of land the same is not true with larger livestock species. The simple fact is that it takes a sizable piece of land to produce the grass-fed beef, the pasture-raised pigs, and the chickens, lamb, and so on that I had just read about. And while Salatin may have inherited his five hundred fifty acres, we were not so fortunate. True, we were acquiring land but it would have to be paid for.

I knew from my business experience that there were many ways other than farming to generate a higher return on capital on the size of investment required to start a sustainable live-stock farm. At the time it seemed highly unlikely that too many people would have the resources to acquire enough land to produce meats humanely and sustainably, and choose to do so. Then again, maximizing return on investment wasn't my aim and wasn't why we moved to the country. Making a living by making life better for others was slowly taking hold of me and becoming my goal. Something was really beginning to resonate with me and a chord had been struck in my soul that rang true and clear. I would keep searching for our path but a new fire was being lit inside me and for the first time in my adult life, it felt right. I was beginning to feel the call to farm and unlike the years I spent behind a desk, this time I knew the reasons. It's real, it's needed, it's right for the animals, it's right for the land, it's right for the environment and it's right for the community. It sounded right, so I said it to myself.

"I want to be a farmer!"

Finally! Something that I can describe to a five-year-old or my mother and they'll both get it instantly. Something that fills me with pride. It was everything that all my prior jobs weren't, which also implied that it was not as financially rewarding as we were accustomed. The big question was, could we make a living at it? I wasn't sure about this since I knew nothing about farming at the time. I probably should have known how difficult it would be but I think I was determined to forge ahead with farming simply because I fell in love with the notion. Still, I wanted an opinion—a sanity check, if you will, to check the calculations of my sophomoric spreadsheet. So I sought out other successful livestock farmers who might be willing to counsel me.

My search for local and sustainable farmers of beef or pork led me to one Georgia farm that I found interesting.

White Oak Pastures, located several hours to the south of us, was a 1,000-acre grass-fed beef farm. According to the website the farm was owned by Will Harris, and the farm had been in his family since the 1860s.

1860s! The days of Abe Lincoln? Are you kidding me? Dang, I was really late to the game!

Will's website described in text and video how he had spent his life as a conventional cattle man but had awakened in mid-life to discover that it made little sense to continue dousing his land with chemicals and trucking cattle a thousand miles away to be processed, only to have them butchered and sent a thousand miles back to his local grocer. So Will, showing great courage and foresight, converted his farm to a certified organic grass-fed operation at a time when virtually no one was doing so. Ah, now here was someone who may be able to help me. And so it was in February 2007 that I picked up the phone and called Will, just as I had tracked down successful entrepreneurs for advice twelve years prior when starting my first business. Like a kid with a plan for a lemonade stand, I enthusiastically told him of my recent readings and asked if he thought I could make a living farming in the same way Pollan and Salatin had described.

"I get that question at least once a week," Will said in the kind of slow southern drawl you would expect to hear from someone at a community theater reading a script for a part in *Gone With the Wind*. Only his accent was the real thing!

"And the answer is *no*," he continued.

Damn!

Will explained how so many people read these books, get their hearts set on moving to the country and then it doesn't work out—for any number of reasons. I thought about what he said and it made sense to me. Indeed, I knew that most businesses fail quickly because they're not properly funded, planned and executed. It always takes more time, money and effort than expected to get a business off the ground and running successfully. Even then, a little luck can't hurt. Well, no one ever tells you it's going to be easy starting a new venture, and you'll always get more people telling you that you *can't* do something than telling you that you *can*. Today people often ask me how to get started with their farm, or any business venture for that matter. The answer I give, I'm sure, rings hollow: "Just do it!" That was the advice that I had to self-prescribe and adhere to as I had done in the past.

I wasn't deterred by what Will said. He wasn't saying that "I" couldn't do it. He was just trying to help someone from making what he thought may become a big mistake. He knew better than anyone that farming successfully is much more difficult than the books make it appear, something I now know he is absolutely correct about. I was grateful for the time he took to talk to me and offer guidance.

Still, if I'm being honest with myself, the fact that it had been suggested that farming may not work for me probably did far more to motivate me to follow this path than an endorsement would have ever done. I don't know why I'm so stubbornly drawn to challenges and obstacles, but if it was a challenge my sub-conscious wanted it should now be permanently satiated by taking on sustainable livestock farming.

I kept thinking about what Will had said and kept flushing out my feelings, trying to separate the emotional draw to the land with the logical nonsense of the idea. About this time Liz and I became aware of Georgia Organics, a local organization that, given our new passion, was of interest to us.

An organization with which we had no previous reason to be acquainted, we learned that Georgia Organics was an Atlanta-based community of like-minded folks concerned with sustainable agriculture in Georgia. One of the many events they had was an annual conference that attracted up to a thousand people. As fate would have it their upcoming tenth anniversary conference was only a few weeks away in early March 2007! I looked over the agenda for the conference and, lo and behold, the keynote speaker was Joel Salatin, the farmer whose book I had just read. Salatin was also hosting an on-farm field day at a small farm near Douglas, where we could see firsthand some of the practices we had read about. Were the stars aligning?

We attended the conference and were like kids in a candy store. It was a whole new world for both of us! So many people were there who shared a concern for sustainable agriculture and who, unlike us at the time, were an active part of the solution. We sat in on some sessions and enjoyed the conference but it was the field day that we longed for. We already felt like we belonged on the farm! The field day was at a small farm that appeared to be mimicking Salatin's model. This wasn't unusual as Salatin is something of a farming icon to many, having worked tirelessly through speeches and writings to cultivate a zealous nationwide following. He has done more than his fair share to inspire others to say "yes" to pasture based farming and "no" to factory farming.

On the farm we saw about a dozen chicken tractors built to Salatin's exact specifications, fronted by Red Angus cows standing belly high in annual ryegrass along with some pigs in the woods. Liz and I were mesmerized. Gone forever, at least from my consciousness, were any thoughts of horses. Here were animals that were in their natural environment living as they evolved to live. Well—for the most part, we thought to ourselves as we walked toward the chicken tractors.

A chicken tractor is a movable pen with an open bottom that is used to confine meat chickens, otherwise known as broilers. A common design calls for the tractors to be ten feet wide by twelve feet long and a height of two feet. Wire poultry netting is run around the perimeter and three quarters of the top is usually covered with metal roofing or the like. Farmers vary their stocking density in the tractors but it's not uncommon to have anywhere from fifty to seventy-five birds in each. Each day you pull the chicken tractor forward by the length of the tractor, or twelve feet, allowing the broilers access to the fresh forage and ensuring that they fertilize the new ground. This type of farming is commonly referred to as "pastured poultry." It was this tractor design we observed for the first time on the field day.

Liz and I stood over the chicken tractors, and coincidentally Will Harris, whom we had never met, walked up beside us. Easy to recognize, he stood out like a legend with his Stetson hat just as we had seen on his website. I introduced myself and we discussed the chicken tractors. We all agreed that the tractors didn't exactly look like a model of nature, what with the chickens having maybe twelve inches of headroom before the hot, metal roofing. It was already quite warm in the first week of March so I couldn't imagine how oppressive the summer sun would be to these South Georgia chicks. They would be hot chicks indeed! Still, the chickens were on pasture, eating grass, and a side effect was that there was no fertility problems as there are in chicken houses.

In commercial chicken houses the bedding and manure must be removed and put somewhere. In a pastured poultry model the manure goes right back on the ground where it belongs. So we had no problem with the pastured poultry part, but we did question whether there was a better alternative than the chicken tractor. We would get to find out for ourselves soon enough.

Near the farmer's house was a brood house where the baby chicks were kept under heat lamps until they were ready to be placed on pasture. Naturally everyone went gaga over this and so did we! Baby chicks, baby pigs, cows—we could really see ourselves living like this, and I suspect we weren't the only ones thinking that way! Or were we? Were we the only crazy ones?

Behind the brood house was a cement slab where the farmer planned to process (that is, kill) chickens that would be sold to consumers. There was much discussion about this as evidently it was illegal in Georgia—or not—to do this. No one seemed to know, although Salatin spoke about a federal law (P.L. 90-492) that allows any farmer in the country to process up to 20,000 chickens per year on a farm. This seemed to us to be a staggering number, and everything was so new to us. Was this even allowed—killing chickens and selling them to customers from a farm? Like most people, we had never even thought about the notion since chickens clearly come only from a grocery store. Still, one of the first lessons we would learn in farming is how purposefully confusing regulations can be. Here was a small farmer wanting to simply process chickens for customers who wanted the freedom to buy directly from him. Was this legal? The feds said yes, the state said no. What's a farmer to do?

Interestingly, we learned a few months later that this small farm on which Salatin held the field day lasted only one year. Evidently they suffered a large loss of poultry due to predators and I was told the farmer returned to the landscaping business.

So much for sustainability, and this clearly gave credence to Will's claim that the farm dreams people pursue are often a mirage. If we were going to farm we wanted to make it work for the rest of our lives. Clearly it was going to be very challenging.

But one thing was becoming very clear. We were beginning to visualize a life that had meaning and we saw an opportunity to heal.

- To heal our new land that had been conventionally farmed, by truly mimicking nature with a model of forage and animal diversity.

- To heal our taste buds, which had been murdered by species homogeneity and long distance transportation of flavorless, unripe food that has to be brined, buttered and salted to produce any flavor worth savoring.

- To heal the animals by raising them in a truly natural setting so that they can act on their evolutionary characteristics.

- To heal the community that had become disconnected from its food supply and from one other.

- To heal our souls by devoting ourselves to an endeavor we so strongly believe in and are so passionate about, and something so fundamental to life itself.

We were beginning to really see it now: how we could play a role and be part of the solution to the problem of producing meat humanely and relearning self-sufficiency skills that were on the verge of extinction. We weren't blind and knew exactly what we were contemplating—that we would raise animals for food. Still, why couldn't they have names, be raised with love and affection while they were here and then be treated with respect and celebration when they nourished us?

What we couldn't see yet was how to make it work, financially. We weren't rich—far from it. We did have some retirement savings that we could invest in the farm to get started, but we'd have to surrender that nest egg and devise a profitable farming model reasonably quickly. Otherwise the model isn't financially viable as the case with the South Georgia farm illustrated, and therefore the farm won't be sustainable. The notions expressed above are noble ideas and all, but not one of them implies that there's any money in farming or that we could even make a living in pursuit of these ideals.

Something that struck a nerve in me early on was how there was such a lack of options for buying meat from animals that were raised naturally and humanely. Like many urban areas, Atlanta had its share of local organic vegetable farmers. Whereas you can produce enough on a small acreage to serve farmers' markets and feed many families, raising livestock requires a large plot of land. Generally speaking, the more notable people doing this were people who had the good fortune of having inherited the land from their family, such as the case with Will Harris at White Oaks Pastures and Joel Salatin at Polyface Farms. In each of their cases they also had the vision to eschew conventional, chemical-based farming methods in favor of a model that treated the land and animals with respect. These were great examples of stewardship, but where would the new diversified livestock farmers come from, and why would they come?

Let me phrase the question differently. Why would someone with the ability to buy a parcel of land large enough to produce meat ethically want to do so, versus developing the land or just hobby farming? After all, it's a never ending responsibility of hard, physically demanding and sometimes dangerous work. If the person's incentive is financial gain then diversified livestock farming may be one of the worst choices they can make. Even if they made the farm successful, how and why would they want to sell it since the successful business would also be their home? Hence there would be no "exit strategy." No, if they were after a return on investment they would seek development or subdivision of the land, which would result in even less land available for farming.

The answer to the question is that the person would have to really, almost altruistically, have a deep desire to make a positive contribution to the community, to the earth and to the earth's inhabitants, whether they have two legs, four legs, toes, hooves, or webbed feet. Farming is just too hard and expensive to do as a hobby and there are, by most people's view, far more enjoyable ways to pass the days. Still, the need is there and somebody needs to do it, and this fact is what pushed me over the edge. We decided that we could and should devote our lives to the land. We had the ability and confidence to trade our priorities, to go from selfish to selfless, to go from consuming earth's resources to preserving earth's resources, to stop complaining about animal welfare to doing something positive about it, to stop feeling entitled and learn to feel more grateful.

To become humbled by nature.

Would we make money? We'll figure it out. That's what I told myself. Today, four years later, I tell myself the same thing. Would we be able to "make it"? We didn't know and sometimes we still don't. But we knew it was the right thing to do. When you know, you know.

Still, there are countless ways we could farm, from vegetables to fruit to row cropping to livestock. We had never been farmers so we had no ties to any particular farming model.

They were all foreign to us and we were starting with a blank slate. Often the toughest sentence to write is the first line on the blank page of a new book. Likewise, as we stared at the blank pages of our farming future the big question for us was, what farming model was right for us?

WORKING FOR A LIVING
BY TIM YOUNG

From a Nature's Harmony Farm Blog Post, April 7, 2010

What do *you* do?

This was the question I used to dread. No matter whether I was at a personal gathering or at a golf course or just chatting with someone I just met, this simple question deserved an equally simple and coherent response.

But I didn't have one. Should I talk about what my job was—what my title was—or should I describe what my business does? As an entrepreneur at the time, I couldn't really separate myself from the business, so I didn't view myself as a CEO. My identity was the business.

"I run a marketing services business," I would say. I had developed a theory that most people don't really care what you do, they just ask "What do you do?" the same way they say "How's it going?." They don't really care. It's just a conversation starter.

So I learned to answer the question with three levels of increasing definition. At the top level I would simply say I run a marketing services business. That would kind of define A) what the business did and B) what my role in it was. Eighty percent of the time that would suffice and the conversation would drift somewhere more interesting, leaving the asker of the question with the feeling that they understood what I did. They didn't.

Then there were the people who had just a little more interest in understanding, so they would probe further.

"A marketing services business? You mean like an agency?" would be their next question.

"Well, kind of," I would reply. "Technology companies outsource marketing services to us."

This often did the trick. Outsourcing was a big word from 1997 or so onward so I would heave that buzzword into the mix with my verbal trebuchet. Surely this would end this boring conversation so we could discuss football, the stock market—or anything else. And it did, pretty much all the time.

Then there were the other five percent. The ones who still didn't "get it" and needed a more detailed explanation.

"What exactly does your company do?"

There was no way around this one.

"Well, large technology companies like Cisco, Intel, SAP, Hewlett Packard and so on outsource their inside sales teams to us."

I could hear myself name-dropping large firms the way someone does who may have seen a couple of celebrities once at a party. "We build relational marketing databases for them and generate sales leads for their global sales team," would be my next scintillating words.

Sometimes this would work, but they'd want to know more about our credibility. So I'd have to confess things like the fact that *Inc.* Magazine had recognized us as the 130th-fastest-growing company in America in 2001 or something like that.

It was these kinds of "accomplishments," whatever that means, that people would cling to. Even my family, the target audience with whom I failed most miserably at conveying what I did, would recite those accomplishments to others with pride, but with failure to convey what I did to whomever they were speaking. At least I somewhat convinced my mother that it was legal. Other than that, they had no clue either.

Why is it that there are so many of these jobs that pay well or provide a living for people, yet they are so unfulfilling? I remember always hating that question, dreading it—"What do you do?" I knew when it was coming and would try to avoid it before it was even asked. True, I had achieved a lot of success at what I did, but I didn't like the measuring stick. Why were we successful? Why was I successful? Who said so? What had I really done? There was always something gnawing inside of me about how I was spending my life and what I was doing. I just didn't know what to do about it.

Today I do. True, I'm no longer a jet-setter (thank the maker for that!) and I'm not flying to Europe every six weeks or so. I don't encounter a lot of people whom I don't already know, as I stay pretty locked up on the farm. But when I do and when we're engaged in a casual conversation, it is with great anticipation that I await the question that society requires they ask. "What do you do?"

"I'm a farmer!" I quickly reply. And I say it with all the pride and enthusiasm I can muster. Whether I'm speaking to my mother, or a five-year-old, they both "get it" immediately. And, true, just like with my previous vocations, I have to answer in increasing detail as they want to know what kind of farming I do. So I proudly tick off cheese-making, natural raising of animals, beekeeping, and so on. They're interested because it's real, it's interesting, and it's fundamental to what we all need.

Today I made cheese for most of the day, and as I turned and salted the wheels of blue cheese I had just made I said to myself, "is there anything more real or more important than this? Producing safe, delicious, nourishment from animals that are living their lives just the way nature intended?"

To me, there isn't. And today, I made cheese.

CHAPTER 4

Eating Animals

Prior to moving to the country I had never been close enough to a cow to touch one. Neither had Liz. Nor had either of us ever looked a rooster in the eyes, presided over the birth of a pig, cuddled a baby chick, pulled a calf, bottle-fed a lamb or chased a turkey with the intention of actually catching it. While we have now checked each of those tasks off the list many times over, when it came to farm animals, we began our farming lives as green as April grass.

How then were we so willingly drawn into a farming life that revolved around livestock? After all, there are countless other farming enterprise options. We love planting and landscaping, so why not create an orchard and market pick-your-own fruits? Most everyone loves fresh fruit and the work involved in that type of farming would allow some time off. Liz in particular loves gardening, so starting a vegetable garden or producing a community-supported agriculture (CSA) program would have also made sense. Yet neither of these options was even contemplated. We decided quickly and decisively that we would raise livestock and, let's be completely frank here, be "meat" farmers. But why?

Of all the decisions we had to contemplate to extricate ourselves from suburbia so that we could devote our lives to farming, choosing to be livestock farmers was the easiest. There were four reasons why this path was so clearly right for us.

For one thing, we love animals. All animals. Imagine, if you will, that a couple is leisurely traversing the countryside meandering through small towns. This couple has a fondness of antique shops or general stores, so the passenger starts "oohing and ahhing" every time he sees one to get the driver's attention. They may not have been even looking for an antique shop but once they see one their fondness for it moves its presence front and center of their consciousness. This is the way Liz and I are with animals.

Let's say that we're driving through a town on a delivery run, since leisurely drives are a rare treat for us nowadays. If Liz sees a pet store it becomes all that she sees. Clearly she knows that we don't need any pets. At any given moment we already have between ten or fifteen dogs, four of which are legitimate "pets." Liz suggests that maybe we can go in for a toy for one of our silkie terriers, conveniently overlooking the fact that they are quite content with any stick on the farm, or our compost pile for that matter, and require no plastic toys from the store. Really she just wants to see the puppies. I do too but try to steer clear, for if the store is sponsoring an adoption event we will no doubt head home with another mouth to feed.

If we're at a store or some public place, I'll be relaying a great story to Liz—or at least what I think is a great story. She'll spot someone with a dog, cat or something fluffy, and her attention is deflected from my oratory masterpiece in favor of those with four legs and fur. One story in particularly illustrates this obsession and how it can almost bite us—literally, I suppose.

The first year we moved to Elberton we were delighted to see that the town had an annual fair. Indeed they had been having this fair each year since 1933 and a permanent fairground is devoted to it, which appears to remains unused for the other fifty weeks of the year. The Elberton 12-County Fair had the usual assortment of rides, games, stage shows and junk food, and there was even a pig racing contest and an exotic animal petting zoo. Like all rural fairs this one had an emphasis on agriculture and featured the best of the town's chickens, roosters, turkeys and pigs. Not having any farm animals of our own yet we lingered through this area for a long time wanting to reach in, touch and hold each animal. Unfortunately, we weren't allowed to.

Also unfortunate was the next stop on our tour. There was a string of vendors set up in the agricultural section, many of which were information providers. Liz didn't notice those. What she did notice was the vendor with a group of people around it marveling at...something. Something that was there, and then it wasn't. Wait! Was that fur? Was that a furry little thing?

Liz is quiet and on the timid side but that didn't stop her from getting to the front row, and fast. This vendor had the tiniest creature we had ever seen. This cute, fuzzy, adorable little animal must have been four or five inches long at most and stayed inside the vendor's shirt pocket. Liz, eyes and mouth agape with wonder, was as captivated by this morsel of a marsupial as Leonardo da Vinci was by Lisa del Giocondo, the famed subject of the "Mona Lisa." The object of her fascination we learned was called a Sugar Glider. We had never heard of such a thing and whereas Liz was engulfed in affection I became overcome with fear that this critter would soon occupy a cradle in our bedroom. The vendor, being skilled at recognizing low-hanging fruit, handed a Sugar Glider to Liz's open hands. A bad case of the pink-and-blue flu had set in and I could tell that Liz needed something new to cuddle. This pink-and-blue flu appeared repeatedly throughout the year, every year, such as when lambs needed bottle-feeding, or at any puppy adoption event. The maternal instincts in Liz are strong—much stronger than I think she realizes. It's joyous watching how compassionately she cares for every living thing, save squash bugs. You do not want to be a squash bug in her garden! But it's also a perpetual reminder that we have no toddlers to cuddle and we continue to seek fulfillment of that longing in other ways.

"We have to get one!" Liz exclaimed. "They're the cutest things I've ever seen."

Rats. I mean, figuratively and literally—this thing looked kind of like a bug-eyed rat.

"OK honey," was my loving stall-tactic of a reply. "Let's go talk about it."

Prying Liz from that table was like pulling a rusty six-inch nail from a railroad tie using nail clippers. Once she was successfully extracted we walked around the fair. Well, I walked, she bounced, much like a Sugar Glider, and it was all we could talk about. In truth I thought about getting it for her birthday, which was only a week away. But I figured we should know something about this alien critter first. Since the fair would be in town for another week, I knew we'd have a chance to get back.

When we got home I went online and researched my new potential roommate. I learned that Sugar Gliders are marsupials native to Australia and New Guinea and can be found in any forest that can sustain them. In particular they are fond of eucalyptus trees. They are also nocturnal, a fact that prompted me to research them further. I searched for reviews and feedback about having Sugar Gliders as pets and what I found gave me hope. Video after video showed unsuspecting owners who, after succumbing to the temptation to buy one, discovered that they stay awake all night screaming an ear-piercing sound. I was saved! A quick copy of the URL and an email to Liz with the loving, supportive message "Here's your new pet honey" brought her back to earth where rationality overcame her. She agreed that maybe it wasn't such a swell idea.

This is how it is with animals and us. While this example illustrates Liz's love for animals, I am no different, having owned at least one dog for every year of my life since I was a boy. I marvel at other animals too and still long for the pet monkey I could never obtain as a child. So it is no surprise that we could not imagine a farming life that did not include lots and lots of animals. The fact that we had no experience with livestock was no more of a deterrent than the fact that we had no experience with a Sugar Glider. The difference was that when we researched cows we concluded that they weren't inclined to keep us up at night. Nor would they share our bedroom, unless of course a calf was really, really cute in Liz's eyes.

Our love of animals brings up an interesting paradox for many people and leads into the second reason why we chose livestock. How could we love an animal and yet kill it for its meat? When it comes to eating meat there is a clear line of division among people. The majority, being products of an environment where meat is cheap and plentiful, think nothing of consuming it. If they do think of it most would be ardent supporters of our right as humans to consume meat and would respect tradition.

Then there are others who, acting mainly out of what they view as compassion for animals, opt to not include meat in their diet. They derive their protein from other sources and take comfort in their perception that no life is harmed in order for them to eat. In reality it's well known that countless lives of insects and mammals are sacrificed to sustain a vegetarian diet. Even though vegetarians often tout perceived health benefits of their diet, in my experience the health benefits are not the reason they originally sought a diet free of meat. Rather the decision was based on moral grounds and it is these values that are put forth as a moral challenge to the world's meat eaters with the claim that it is unethical to eat meat. If you look closely at the reasons they cite they indeed have a point worthy of consideration, as the factory-farmed animals that give their lives for our dining pleasure endure, by most definitions, horrid existences. Let's examine them.

Before enjoying those eggs for breakfast, consider that laying hens are crowded in battery cages so tightly that they can't lie down or stretch their wings. Ever. At a stocking density of less than forty-eight square inches per bird, almost five hundred hens could be crammed into an average coat closet. Close your eyes and imagine that life for a second. Jut so we can have cheap eggs. Even though humankind has domesticated animals for thousands of years the animals still retain genetic instincts to do what comes naturally to their species. And so the hen has a strong urge to stretch out, roost and just take a dust bath. She'll enjoy none of these most elementary desires in her short life, which will last about one year. At that point she will have been allowed to lay her last egg and will earn the unflatteringly intuitive title of a "spent hen." Off to slaughter she goes, leaving her less fortunate cellmates behind.

Many people are finally becoming familiar and quite alarmed by the horrid existences that laying hens are forced to endure in battery cages. Still, most people are quite unaware that for every laying hen, which by definition is a female, a male was hatched out. The male, having the misfortune of belonging to a laying breed, has neither the ability to lay eggs nor the ability to gain weight quickly and efficiently as meat birds do. Thus, his life concludes on the day it begins as more often than not he is ground up alive. This heart-wrenching atrocity is something I delve into in more detail in chapter 8.

The laying hen's cousin, the broiler chicken, also lives in a crowded chicken, house albeit on a filthy floor with up to 30,000 other broilers. The life of a broiler could begin on January 1 and a reflection in the mirror would confirm to the broiler that he was indeed a cute, fuzzy little yellow ball of fluff curious to what the world had in store for him. This would likely be the best day of the broiler's life, for while his mind had the evolutionary curiosity of a chicken his body had been re-programmed by humans to do very unnatural things. Like for instance to grow so remarkably fast that his legs would fail, by design, before he reached fifty days of age. Not that he will live that long, as most broilers are bred to grow from that yellow fuzzy cotton ball of a chick to almost five pounds in about thirty-nine days, at which time they are "harvested" for our chicken sandwiches. That's if an industrial breed chicken lives to thirty-nine days. Up to thirty percent of them do not, as heart attacks and respiratory problems from the rate of growth run rampant.[2]

Since consumers like their chicken sandwiches to be plump, "Broilers 2.0" were further redesigned to not only grow alarmingly fast but to put that growth precisely in the breast area. They didn't need it as much in the legs and indeed would be environmentally discouraged from exercise anyway, given the density with which they are packed in confinement. Today's designer chicken aims at meeting the requirements of the finicky American public, which demands a plump breast (from all species, as it turns out). Why accept what nature gives us with gratitude when it can so easily be improved upon? Indeed, size does seem to matter.

The broiler that began its life on January 1 may have made it to mid-February and thus only experienced one season in life. A horrid, miserable winter that seemed to last an eternity rather than a mere thirty-nine days. Not that it was cold, as the climate-controlled conditions and perpetual artificial sunshine ensured the bird's comfort and forced it to stay alert so that it could eat up to twenty-three hours per day. The broiler's last view of this world would result in his only effort at flight and a poor one at that, as handlers hurriedly and indifferently fling the birds into metal cages that transport them to slaughter. Who knows what the broiler actually contemplates at this point, if anything, but perhaps he is eager for the end to arrive. Surely something better lies ahead.

Pigs fare no better. Commercially reared sows live their lives comfortable with the knowledge that the earth is in fact made of metal and cement, yet question why the maker gave them a snout and an intense desire to dig in the concrete, which they can't do. Surely the sows, or mother pigs, further question why the desire was implanted to turn around or be with their young when both of these "luxuries" are denied. A farrowing crate only allows the sow to face one way while her piglets are kept on the outside just close enough to reach her teats. For their part they'll only have this limited access to their mother for a few weeks before being removed, where the misery of their life really begins.

If they're unlucky enough to be a male pig they will endure excruciating castration at a few days old without any anesthesia. The reason has to do with the perception of boar taint, which unleashes itself as an offensive odor during cooking meat from an intact, or un-castrated, male pig. Boar taint is associated with two compounds produced in the live male pig: androsterone and skatole. Androsterone is a steroid produced by the testes and concentrated in the salivary glands. There it is converted to a pheromone involved in eliciting sexual behavior in gilts and sows during the mating process. Androsterone is also deposited in the fat tissue and can be released in response to heat during cooking, thus contributing to boar taint.[3]

Skatole is a compound produced by bacteria in the hindgut of the boar. It is absorbed across the intestinal wall into the blood stream, metabolized by the liver and may be excreted or absorbed into fat tissue where it <u>may</u> cause boar taint.[4]

I underlined the word "may" in the last sentence, since the obvious conclusion is that it also "may not" cause boar taint. The controversy surrounding castration is one of humane treatment. In North American swine production castration is essentially universal whether the pig be on an industrial or small family farm. In the UK and Ireland, for welfare reasons, pigs are not castrated. Additionally, legislation was passed in Norway and Switzerland banning castration of pigs beginning in 2009, while the majority of male pigs in Spain and Portugal are not castrated.[5]

In fact, both McDonald's and Burger King in the Netherlands announced that they would no longer sell products containing pork from castrated pigs.[6]

All of this raised a simple question in our minds. Why are we needlessly and painfully castrating pigs?

Then there are the cows, who in some respects have it worst of all. Whereas the turkey, hen, broiler and pig only know one existence, that of climate-controlled confinement, virtually all cows in this country are born on pasture and nurse their mother. Except for male dairy calves, which are often promptly removed and milk-fed in close confinement for the veal market, calves often enjoy the pleasures of pasture under their hooves, sunshine on their backs and a breeze in their face. They experience much of the joy that any cow could reasonably hope for in life.

Then, in an instant, it changes.

When the calf reaches weaning age, usually around six months, it is separated from its mother and the land for the first time and put on a livestock trailer. There is little time for the trauma of that separation to set in as the calf is quickly unloaded at a sale barn where it is driven into a ring to confront what for it is surely a horrifying sight. Crowds of humans are in front waving their arms frantically with a loud auctioneer seated behind mooing in a foreign tongue. Just as the calf takes in the scene the gate opens and it makes a break for it, finding instead of an open pasture another trailer. This double-deck trailer will take the calf on its last journey, a two-day trip, where, upon unloading, it will be greeted by thousands upon thousands of other cows all standing knee-deep not in lush grass, but in muck. The calf quickly learns the new routine and finds the only source of sustenance available, delivered in the form of a daily ration of thirty-two pounds of feed. The feed is predominantly grain, something the calf has never tasted before, but also includes what is deemed to be a healthy dose of antibiotics, growth stimulants, chicken litter, protein supplements and even pot scrubbers. Yes, pot scrubbers are sometimes fed to cows in confinement, as is chicken litter, excrement and all, with not a blade of grass in sight.

The high-energy corn diet the calf is fed is far more acidic than the bovine's rumen has evolved to naturally tolerate. The rumen, with a capacity of approximately forty-five gallons (imagine nine 5-gallon buckets) is essentially a fermentation vat in which bacteria convert plant cellulose into proteins and fats. I consider it an evolutionary marvel how a ruminant can convert grass into milk and meat that in turn provides nourishing sustenance to humans. Cows evolved over millennia harvesting their own grasses, not being force-fed grains, so the high-energy diet forced upon it increases the acidity of the rumen just enough to create a hospitable environment for such dangers as e.coli 0157:H7 which can then be transferred to humans.

Back at the feedlot, I have no way of knowing if the calf reflects on where it is while at the feedlot and how it came to be there, but the calf can be assured that its best days lie behind.

Perhaps then you can see how vegetarians and animal rights activists can make an argument that there are indeed ethical and moral consequences to consuming meat. So why then do Liz and I feel so strongly that it is not only ethical, but also critical that we raise animals for human consumption? If we chose to not eat meat, one problem for us was that the decision, without question, would represent a major deviation from the natural history of how humankind evolved. Here we were aspiring to farm naturally in accordance with nature so that animals could live as they evolved and express their natural instincts. Did that not include we humans as well?

Over millennia, humankind subsisted partly, but consistently, on a diet of protein from animals that lived natural lives. The eaters needed no label to tell them that. For sure this diet also included nuts, berries, leaves, mushrooms, fish and whatever edible substances were found naturally in their local environment. So in my view it's fair to put forth the moral challenge that meat should not be consumed, but it's equally fair to consider a non-debatable, simple truth: humankind evolved to the point we are at now by consuming protein from animals that lived or were raised naturally (not factory-farmed animals). Any manmade deviation from that evolutionary trajectory is clearly an attempt to assert unnecessary influence or control over our natural environment, rather than respecting, honoring and living within it.

I myself had once lived a vegan lifestyle for six months, mainly out of curiosity. Liz toyed with a vegan lifestyle as well but in the end we both found that we just plain enjoy animal protein. Moreover, we felt like our bodies needed it. The simple truth is that my body "feels" better when my diet includes meat, seafood, dairy and eggs than when it is excluded.

Having clearly decided that we enjoy meat and dairy, let me turn my attention to the core question raised not only by animal rights activists, but by ourselves as animal lovers. Is it morally ethical to consume animals?

As I mentioned, Liz contemplated a vegan lifestyle after reading about the miserable lives animals endure in confined animal feeding operations, or CAFOs. It seems so unreal to me that there was a time when we were blissfully unaware of what a CAFO was or that the animals that gave their lives for us lived such utterly tragic existences. How could we have been so blind? Like most people in our society we had become unknowing participants in an industrial food system. This wasn't voluntary on our part any more than was learning the English language. It was the environment in which we were raised and like most we never questioned it, at least not for a long time. Naiveté and ignorance can be reasonable excuses to engage in activities that more enlightened souls may see as reprehensible. However, once a person gains knowledge is it not their responsibility to do something about it and accept the moral, emotional, societal and physical consequences of their decision?

In one very important way, farmers such as Liz and I are completely united with animal rights activists. We all share a complete and utter contempt for industrial factory farming methods. Herein lies the fuzzy or gray area. Upon close examination of the ethical reasons so often put forth that form the foundation of why humans should not eat meat, I find that the compelling indictment is not against eating meat *per se*, but rather an indictment against factory farming methods and how animals are raised.

Moreover, we share another common trait that we act on in diametrically opposed ways. That trait is a complete love of and respect for animals, expressed by animal rights supporters' wish that no meat be consumed, with the obvious implication that no farm animal will experience life at all; and expressed by us as wanting to ensure an animal can live and natural life, even though that life will one day end and nourish us. Ensuring that animals can have the opportunity at a natural life is the third reason why we chose to farm livestock.

Think about the scenario I described before for the animals raised in industrial settings. Let's look at just one of those examples now through a different lens.

A one-year old Ossabaw Island sow, Candy, walks through the woods carrying privet in her mouth. The privet grows abundantly in the woods in which she lives and Candy freely rips it from the ground, although she has no interest in eating it. She slowly circles, looking for just the right spot, and places the privet on the ground. There's a mound of it now and more is being brought over by other sows with whom she has lived her entire life.

Candy uses her long snout and begins digging in the cool summer dirt to form a depression. The depression is about the size of her body and, once formed, allows her to lie down and cover herself with the privet. She receives no instructions on how or why to build a nest other than the genetic instructions imprinted upon her through countless generations of ancestors who enjoyed living natural lives. Indeed this is Candy's first gestation and she's never felt this way before. Unlike sows raised in factory farms, for whom maternal instincts are undesirable and therefore have been bred out, Candy somehow instinctively knows what to do. Covered by privet, a passerby would be completely unaware of the five baby piglets that have emerged one by one over the course of an hour. The babies have their own instincts and find their way to the mother's teats for nursing, which have been perfectly presented due to the slope of the depression she formed, allowing her to lie on her side. Candy summons the piglets using a vocal call that she has never uttered before. A deep grunting sound that imprints upon the piglets resulting in a bond that will unite them throughout their time together.

Of the five piglets, three are male and two are female. This makes little difference as all five will live with the sow until they are weaned naturally, which generally occurs at two or three months, and the males will never be castrated. Nor will the piglets have rings put in their noses, their tails docked or their ears notched, as is common with most confinement pigs. These pigs know nothing of those things; they are simply pigs in nature's landscape. Day after day they will run, sleep, eat and play in the woods with mother and the other Ossabaws in their tribe. They are unacquainted with cement, huts and crates, but do know of caring humans who make sure they have clean water and occasionally bring them yummy treats such as whey and give them a good scratching. Other times they are free to hunt for their own food, something they rejoice in as they tear apart felled trees looking for grubs, crunching loudly on acorn or hickory nuts, or devouring persimmons that have ripened and fallen to the ground.

After the mother has weaned the piglets the male and female piglets are separated and each joins other male or female piglets that they know in a larger group. They miss their mother for a time just as we all do when life weans us, but they enjoy their freedom and the friendships they've known all along. The humans still bring whey and water and the pigs root through the dirt forming wallows to make mud so they can cool themselves off, since they have no sweat glands. They sleep when and where they want, eat what they can find, and form a strong bond with the rest of their group. Life is good.

One of Candy's fifteen-month old piglets, now a full-grown boar having seen each of the seasons of the year at least once, excitedly jumps onto a trailer with several others his size, eager to consume the whey waiting for him. The door closes and the trailer moves to its destination, where the door opens. Although the location looks different, the pigs are eager to exit. Their feet feel hard ground—concrete, for the first time. They calmly walk down a chute as no one is pushing them, until they reach a small room. They don't realize they are standing on a platform, but they are, and the door shuts behind them. The pigs have lived their entire life together, and so may take comfort in the fact that they are with one another as the platform descends into a carbon dioxide chamber. Just as their lives began together, so it now ends. Indeed it is not a good moment for pigs, but is likely the only bad day they have ever experienced.

We should be so lucky in that regard.

Unlike the factory-farming example, I purposely took this illustration through the entire life cycle of the pig. As farmers we understand death all too well and our eyes are wide open when we take the animals we love to the mechanism that will turn them from pig into pork. We obviously love these animals very much, so how could we kill them? Beyond the fact that, as stated previously, we feel the need for animal protein, the answer is simple. These rare Ossabaw pigs that we just slaughtered as humanely as we could would have never experienced one breath of life had we not only granted the opportunity to them, but also worked to cultivate a market of consumers willing to ensure the survival of their breed by, ironically, eating them. They enjoyed life to the fullest and we enjoyed our time with them greatly. The same example is true for the slow-growing heritage turkeys we raise on pasture who would never know life if we did not create a market for their meat at Thanksgiving.

In my view it is far less humane and morally unethical to deny life at all, as animal rights supporters propose, than to grant life and provide the conditions for animals to fully express their genetic characteristics and instincts. Yet if animal rights supporters had their way the world would be vegan and every animal granted a beautiful life in our world would be nonexistent in theirs. For us the right decision is to abolish and condemn factory farming, not ethical meat consumption.

In the end, who are the real animal rights supporters then? The ones who aspire to deny life or the one who aspire to grant each animal a natural life that will ultimately end?

Even though we support meat consumption, Liz and I also advocate eating less meat. That's an intriguing suggestion coming from "meat farmers" but I suspect most of us would agree that we don't need all the meat we're consuming in this country. Certainly humans didn't arrive at our current stage of evolution by, pardon the pun, "pigging out" on so much meat over millennia. For our part we enjoy small portions of meat and during the summer eat quite little of it. Just as backyard gardeners have discovered the real taste of a tomato, we found that we savor a small amount of wonderfully flavorful naturally raised meat rather than the gluttonous supply of flavorless, factory farmed meat.

Beyond our perceived need for meat and our desire to give animals a great life, a fourth reason we chose to farm livestock was because we needed their help if we were to restore health to the land we now cared for. In early 2007, as I walked among the fields of what is now Nature's Harmony Farm, my eyes fixated on all that was wrong. Among the bulging clumps of fescue were expansive areas of hard, bare ground, large areas of briars and brambles, and a ubiquitous display of weeds that even I as a novice farmer could recognize as being unpalatable to a cow. Even though I had visited at a rare wet time the crunch underfoot in the fields was much louder than walking on the sticks in the woods. These fields had been disked, tilled and planted each year so that cows could have winter forage. Now that the ground had been untouched for over a decade, unpalatable and indeed poisonous weeds had taken the place once occupied by lush forage, making it far from picturesque or worthy of supporting animal life. I wanted to heal that land and in exchange I wanted that land to heal my soul and to provide nourishment that would sustain others.

We called our county extension agent who promptly recommended that we burn the pastures and plant again. He meant literally burn them. This would be the first in a string of recommendations that we would receive from various authorities that made no sense to us and as a result we chose to not follow. We were pleased a few months later when this agent moved on and was replaced by an agent who proved to be very helpful and enthusiastic about our plans.

Liz and I read extensively about improving organic matter and pasture quality through grazing, particularly rotational grazing. We read works written over a half century ago by Sir Albert Howard and Andre Voisin, the 1959 author of what would become a classic conservation book entitled *Grass Productivity*. Voisin made a compelling case for rotational grazing and putting grazing livestock with grass at the right stage of forage development for a limited time. Rotational grazing simply means frequently moving grazing animals such as sheep and cows from one paddock to another, with the goal being to allow them to eat or trample forages in their paddock without having time to take a second bite of the plant. When a cow bites a plant, the plant responds by shedding a corresponding amount of root mass that will, owing to the wonderful life within the soil, become humus and organic matter. Above ground the plant responds to the cow's attack by growing quickly, like a teenager. The goal is to keep the grazer off the plant until the plant growth nears the top of its growth curve and graze it again just before the growth plateaus and the plant lignifies.

Management-intensive grazing is the same thing as rotational grazing except that the cows are moved very frequently, generally once a day. We had never had cows of course, so at first the idea of moving them every day seemed a little daunting. Others who were practicing this form of grazing, about whom we had read in publications such as *Graze* and the *Stockman Grass Farmer*, made it seem doable and so this was the path we committed to. Our initial vision was to graze multiple species of animals on fields that had multiple species of forage as we thought this model of biodiversity best approximated what is observed in nature. While a monoculture such as a field of coastal Bermuda grass or tulips may appear beautiful to some, where in nature do you see prairies of only one forage or wildflower species? That unnatural approach made little sense to us.

To best achieve our goal of animal diversity we let go of the idea of having a horse and instead visualized having grazers such as cows and sheep; birds such as turkeys, hens, broilers and ducks; and pigs. Pigs, even though they would live in the woods, would help us to restore health to the pastures. Some of the most menacing intruders in our fields were locust trees, yellow crownbeard and privet, all of which encroached from the woods. Rotating pigs around the pasture/woodlot borders would ensure they would keep the undesirable forages for grazing in the woods rather than allowing uninvited access to the pastures. Raising pigs, which we never contemplated when we abruptly bought the land, would provide another benefit. Of the original seventy-two acres we began with, approximately twenty were primarily hardwoods.

Factory farming is all about changing the environment; clearing land, putting up chicken houses, swine houses and feedlots, bringing animals in, importing feed, creating a pollution problem at the factory farm and creating a fertility problem on the land. The fertility problem is a result of farmers cutting hay or growing grain to be transported to the factory farms for feed, thereby robbing nutrients from a land already void of the animals needed to replenish fertility. In such a scenario, the land loses fertility and topsoil, year after year, thereby rendering the model ecologically unsustainable. We looked at our land and tried to visualize how it could best be used as it was. The woodlot's cornucopia of forages including grasses, mushrooms, acorns, mulberries, persimmons and downed trees with grubs was a perfect habitat for pigs. We selected pigs not because we necessarily wanted pigs or because the consumer market wanted pork. We selected them because the land needed services that they were best suited to render. We repeated this process in all areas of the farm, giving the land what it called for and what it called for was the symbiotic partnership it had historically enjoyed with animals.

To accomplish this my role as farmer would be more akin to an orchestra conductor than what is normally thought of as a livestock farmer, and this notion struck me as a worthy lifetime pursuit. There are countless ways I could choose to go through life. Given the choice between relaxing on the beach and working hard to make a difference in the lives of others, I'd prefer the latter. Farming gave me that opportunity. The lives of others I am referring to take many forms, and includes:

- Consumers, who want nutritious, humanely raised meats;
- Animals, who deserve the chance to live their lives as nature intended;
- The community, who would benefit from the security of a local food shed; and,
- The soil and the environment, which must be treated with utter respect or they will ultimately unleash utter disaster on the perpetrators. Namely, us.

As we tirelessly picked up truckloads of rocks from the fields, removed old fence lines and breathed new life into the farm, we eagerly anticipated our animal friends finally joining us and rejoicing in their new freedom. They would have to help us learn how to farm, and we would be here to help them learn how to live natural lives with minimal human support.

We reflected that in a remarkable six-month period from October 2006 to April 2007, we had completely changed the course of our lives. We had stepped out of our comfort zone, walked away from everything we knew and understood in suburban America, and immersed ourselves in a strange new world. We were eager and thought we were ready to ring the bell that signaled that the farm was open. School was about to begin, but neither the animals nor we were prepared for the tests that nature had in store.

RADIO HOMEMAKERS
BY LIZ YOUNG

From a Nature's Harmony Farm Blog Post, Dec 23, 2009

We all need inspiration. I'm hoping that I have found some in a podcast I recently heard with Evelyn Birkby. I don't know how Tim finds these hidden jewels, but he always seems to know what I need. I haven't blogged in over a month and lately I've tried, but I just stared at a blank screen before closing it out and giving up. It's not because I don't have things to share, but it's because I haven't had the energy or patience to deal with the consequences of what I say. The overwhelming majority of people who read and comment on our blog are very supportive and encouraging, but every now and then we get some unsolicited criticism that sends me over the edge. Whether it be from vegetarians who call us "evil" or fellow farmers who say we are doing things all wrong, the intolerance I feel from some of their comments has been enough to make me want to hide!

Well, hearing Evelyn has reminded me of why we blog in the first place. We put our stories out there in order to share. When we started farming we wanted to share our adventures. We also wanted to share our passion with the hopes of inspiring others to follow their dreams. As our eyes opened to the industrial food system, we have also shared what we have learned and learned that sharing what we do is the only way to ensure complete transparency for our customers. So in the end, we farm the way we farm and live the way we live, and it is not for anyone to judge. I would not seek out a vegetarian and criticize their choices nor would I confront a farmer who chooses to raise their animals in a way that I do not agree with. We will make the world a great place by building people up, not by breaking them down.

The podcast "Sustainable Agriculture Spotlight" with Evelyn Birkby attempts to see what lessons we might learn from an old-time farmer that we could apply to sustainable agriculture today. It speaks about how over two-thirds of small family farms have disappeared, and with them has gone much of their homesteading and sustainable agricultural knowledge. In this podcast, Evelyn, who was ninety years old, shares her stories of being a farm wife and a radio homemaker. You'll fall in love with her the minute you hear her voice! She talks about how during the 1940s "radio homemakers" were basically farm wives who would share information on the AM radio waves. When Evelyn first got married she admits that she had no idea how to be a farm wife and therefore solicited help from her neighbors. Her neighbors would call in to offer encouragement, advice, recipes, etc. Evelyn learned that during an era where farm wives did not get much credit, they were actually very powerful and knowledgeable people. It was the sharing and swapping of stories and experiences that built farm communities.

During the podcast I was enthralled with the nostalgia and entertained by Evelyn's memories, but I was also envious of what the radio homemakers had going. They had a community of people, loyal listeners and contributors, whose sole purpose was just to share and help. There have been many times that I have found the virtual sustainable agriculture and homesteading communities to be very supportive and to share tidbits of their experience with no strings attached. This is a wonderful thing that I want to see more of and so it's only right for me to continue contributing in ways that I can. I love hearing about how someone has made bacon for the first time or had a successful garden harvest. It's inspiring to hear when people have connected with their food and the land. And it's so helpful to hear advice from people who have tried some of the lost arts of food preservation or natural rearing of livestock. So please share!

It's easy to write a comment on our blog, so give me your best homesteading or sustainable farming tip. Share what you've learned about raising animals, living on a farm, cooking, etc. Building a local food community, a farming community, or just a community of neighbors all starts with sharing. And listen to Evelyn if you need a little inspiration!

Here—I'll start.

One thing that I like to do is to make our own butter. I grew up on margarine and never knew how good butter tasted. Then, when we got a home milk cow I made butter and realized that I never knew how great home-made butter tasted! It's easy to do and all you need is heavy cream and a food processor. Just put the cream in the processor and turn it on. In a few minutes you see the consistency change and the butter will separate out from the buttermilk. Pour off the buttermilk and use it to make some biscuits! Wash the butter by putting it in a jar, covering it with ice water, then giving it a good shake. Pour off the milky water and repeat until the water runs clear. Now you've got butter! Try mixing the soft butter with different flavors like honey or garlic or add some herbs. It's a great way to learn about the qualities of milk and to get some gourmet butter suited just to your taste!

PART 2

Reconnecting Animals With the Land and People With Their Food

CHAPTER 5

Pig Tales

Under a damp, gray November sky, Liz and I paced anxiously in the north pasture. Light was fading fast, and we were nervous. Today the first animals were scheduled to join us, and life at Nature's Harmony Farm would officially begin.

Several months prior, we had decided to start simultaneously with both pigs and beef cows. The cows would be coming from farms in Ohio and Oklahoma later that month, but the pigs, freshly weaned, were ready now.

We had settled on the Berkshire breed of pig. Essentially a black pig with white feet and some white spotting, the Berkshire began in the 1700s, ironically as a red pig with a few black spots. This pig from the English shire of Berks was instantly recognized to have superior carcass qualities, earning it favor among the dining élite of the day. This reputation persists to this day and indeed it is now called Kurobuta (Black Hog) pork in Japan where it is revered the way Kobe beef is. In the U.S., Berkshire pork is highly sought after by chefs due to its intramuscular marbling, or fat, which results in a deliciously flavorful dining experience. Given this stellar reputation the Berkshire seemed like a fine first-draft pick for the Nature's Harmony Farm team. Today eight little piggies would be joining us from a Kentucky farm. Only they were late and as rookie farmers we were understandably nervous about receiving them in the dark.

Liz and I had spent the day setting up a wooded paddock using portable fencing, which consists of step-in posts, electrified poly-wire and a portable battery to keep the fence hot, or electrified. Only a few months before, we had known nothing of portable fencing and rechargeable batteries but had visited a farmer in South Carolina who kindly showed us how they work. Since we would move all animals frequently around the farm in a complex rotational grazing model, our farm would need to revolve around the concept of mobility. Everything would need to be portable and impermanent. These electric fences would be a new experience for the pigs too so they would have to be trained to it. We had recently installed a woven-wire perimeter fence around the entire farm and the permanent fence formed the back of the paddock, so we felt secure with that.

The pig's paddock was equipped with a water trough and a float valve, which was connected to a garden hose that joined a local spigot. The spigot was part of a system of in-ground PVC we had recently buried stretching 8,000 feet around the farm. This way we would always be within 250 feet of a tap carrying fresh water from our newly drilled well, thereby ensuring a supply of fresh water to our new friends. We had secured a couple of small, second-hand two-hole pig feeders that now stood in the middle of the paddock filled to the brim with feed. We were ready for life to begin on the farm.

As darkness fell two headlamps finally snaked towards us down the half-mile driveway. We flashed our lights and guided the pickup truck across the pasture to our specific location. Chris, a Kentucky farmer with a lifetime of experience raising Berkshires, got out and opened the rear hatch on his truck. Inside were six gilts and two young boar pigs that were about to become barrows. A gilt is a female pig that has yet to mature to breeding age, at which time she will become a sow. These females, now about five months of age each, would be bred at nine months to become our first sows at about a year of age. The gestation cycle of a pig is 114 days, which is easy to remember as five months, three weeks, three days.

The two male pigs were part of the same litter so we did not want to breed them to the gilts, so we would be getting a Berkshire male from another breeder for that purpose. In our presence these males were about to become barrows, or castrated male pigs. We were about to get our hands dirty.

It's hard not to wince or get squeamish just saying the word "castrate," and we were uneasy about the whole thing. We had witnessed the procedure once before while visiting a farmer in North Carolina who raised Ossabaw Island pigs. Every farmer told us that male pigs must be castrated lest the meat become permeated with boar taint. Still we were uncertain about this and so I had asked Chris to do this procedure with me.

Most farmers castrate males at about three to five days of age when they can be handled more easily, but these male pigs had been weaned and were already quite large, about forty pounds each. In the darkness, I reached in and grabbed the first pig I had ever grabbed by the rear legs and held it upside down with its head dangling near my knees facing away from me.

This did not please the young male who voiced an ear-piercing screech that must have been audible for miles around.

The sheer strength of such a young pig caught me off guard as it flung its legs, head and torso through the air like a pinched balloon just freed of the air that filled it. Pulling the pig against my body seemed like it would be a mistake as it would provide a launch pad for the pig's strong legs. Still, I knew I couldn't let the pig go so I pulled it tightly to me and squeezed its head between my thighs. I pulled my arms apart to spread his hind legs, presenting the scrotal area to Chris who stood at the ready with a knife and blue spray to treat the wound afterwards.

It happened fast.

Chris took his free hand and pushed the testicle against the scrotum to identify it. A quick slit was carefully made and the testicle was pushed through. Rather than cutting the testicle free it was literally stretched and pulled through the opening, severing the cord that held it intact, a process that just seemed wrong to me. Chris explained that this results in less bleeding and faster recovery than cutting the cord and indeed we had witnessed this same method in North Carolina. Still, I didn't like it.

With the blue spray applied liberally the newly anointed barrow was placed on the ground where he, surprisingly, went about his business as if nothing had happened. He had a stubby little tale so we named him Stub. He would now be joined by Duke, on whom we quickly and just as unpleasantly repeated the castration procedure.

With the dirty work behind us we picked up the young gilts and introduced the family of eight to their paddock. Pigs do not possess excellent eyesight but do possess a remarkable sense of smell. Thus, being pigs, they sniffed around and explored their new environment. Chris said his goodbyes and continued on his journey leaving Liz and me alone in the dark with our new babies.

From this moment on, we were farmers.

Our house was still five months away from being completed so we had to drive an hour each way when we needed to be at the farm. From now on we would need to be there very frequently. We weren't about to head home for the night until we were sure the piggies would be OK. Could they even see at night? Would they know where to sleep? Would they be afraid? It's kind of ridiculous thinking such thoughts now but that's what we wondered then.

The paddock was very large so they had plenty of room to roam. Arriving in the dark at a new home after such a long journey must have been at least a little traumatic. We got in with them and squatted down hoping to comfort and reassure anyone requiring or desiring attention. One of the female pigs in particular, a larger one, was a little skittish. She would run back and forth through the woods in the paddock. Not that we could see her as she was a black mass moving in the darkness, but we could hear her. In the distance we heard her squeal—and then we heard nothing. Liz and I jumped to our feet and sprinted in that direction with a powerful flashlight illuminating our path, trying desperately not to trip over roots and downed trees in the blackness. We saw the electric fence vibrating as if the wind had blown it.

We realized the vibration was a result of a pig having just run through it.

Our pig.

"Oh no!" Liz exclaimed. "That pig got out!"

We hurdled the two-foot high fence and sprinted after the pig along the woven-wire perimeter fence. At this point I realized that we were running toward an opening in the fence where a gate would later go. The pig's paddock was a couple of hundred yards from the opening so it wasn't critical that the gate was installed prior to their arrival. Or so I thought. As I was running I desperately wished the gate was already there, but it wasn't. We saw the pig running along the fence line ahead of us and, not wanting to have our worst fears go unrealized, she turned right, went through the opening and ran into the black wilderness. I ran after her but just behind the woven-wire fence was a steep slope that bottomed out at Sally's creek, which held flowing water and slippery rocks at this time of year. Barely navigable if you're a four-legged pig and non-negotiable if you're me. Liz and I stopped, out of breath, and stared at one another.

"What do we do?" we both said.

What we did was run back to make sure the other pigs were still there, which they were. We discussed our plan of attack. I searched the woods for a long time, stalking, calling, listening and shining the light, all to no avail. If you ever find yourself in the woods searching for a pig I can assure you that the call "Here piggy piggy" is vastly overrated as a means of luring a pig.

Liz was searching too but was half frozen by the fear of what else might be out there in the night chasing her! Every rustle of leaves or cracking of a stick would conjure images in Liz's mind of encroaching coyotes, bears, bobcats, and perhaps even man-eating lions. She wondered what in the world we had gotten ourselves into and silently longed for the comfort of a day spa back in suburbia.

There was no sign of Birdie, a name Liz had hastily bestowed in the darkness to the jail bird of a pig who had just earned the legendary status of being the first animal to escape from the, apparently, very minimal security prison at Nature's Harmony Farm. After two hours of waiting and watching the seven remaining pigs settle down to sleep, we finally decided we needed sleep ourselves.

We headed home as failures. We had been farmers for only a few hours and what had we accomplished other than losing a pig?

As I drove home I pondered our loss in financial terms. This began an ongoing habit of running calculations through my mind in an endless pursuit of financially sustainable farming models. I figured that this escaped gilt would have given us, on average, eight pigs per litter twice a year for at least five years. Based on this estimate we just lost eighty piglets directly and far more if you calculate that we could have bred many of those to expand our herd or flock or, whatever you call it, of pigs. We later learned that a group of pigs may be called a drove, herd or a mob. Mob sounded right to me. Still, at $500 per pig that was $40,000 in gross revenue over the next five years, gone in the darkness.

The next morning we were on the road before dawn so that we could check on the pigs and see if there was any sign of Birdie and indeed if the other pigs were still there. Upon arrival at the farm we saw pigs running in the paddock and breathed a quick sigh of relief. Seeing the seven little pigs filled us with a sense of solace normally reserved for a parent who realizes that their newborn infant is safe and sound their first morning at home. Seven wasn't as good as eight but it was way better than zero!

Liz demonstrated right away the keen and compassionate eye she has for animal welfare. She noticed Duke and Stub bleeding from their scrotal area although they appeared fine otherwise. This discovery put her into a panic, which in turn put me into a panic. I called Chris and relayed the information only to be reassured that it was normal. Liz accepted my information suspiciously. It turned out that Chris was right.

Our faith in ourselves as farmers momentarily restored, we walked among our knee-high friends to see how the rest were adjusting. What we saw at the rear of the paddock got our hearts racing again.

Just on the other side of the woven-wire fence, there was Birdie!

After we had left the prior night and everything settled down, evidently Birdie found her way back to her family and slept just outside the fence. This welcome sight taught us an important lesson about pigs, particularly their desire to be together as part of the herd. Liz and I sprang into action, running outside the fence with hopes of driving Birdie along the fence back through the opening, but she was smarter and more agile than we. Round and round we went, tripping over everything, as Birdie just stayed within sight of her family, but out of our reach.

We scratched our heads until Liz had the idea to prop up the woven wire fence and create an opening under which Birdie could crawl. The plan was to put some food there and entice Birdie to come back through. After rigging up this egress from the wilderness Liz and I split up on each side of the opening by about twenty yards so that Birdie could come between us. We waited patiently as Birdie, wary of our presence, was slow to do our bidding. But do our bidding she did as her nose led her to the opening at the fence. Once there she craved the food and companionship on the other side. Liz and I ruffled through the leaves and walked up behind her. Birdie thrust herself through and we quickly pulled down the fence, celebrating the genius of our idea and our victory as farmers. The piggies were back together again!

A Pig's Life

Pigs are definitely at home in the woods. From a vantage point eighteen inches above the ground a pig, the ultimate omnivore, sees a treasure trove of organic material beckoning closer inspection. A downed tree that for humans is a nuisance to step over or around, holds a bounty of insects, grubs and tasty treats that are easily and joyfully extracted, if you are a pig. Roots, tubers, grasses, nuts, eggs, lizards, frogs and even snakes are all part of the pig's diet and all are available for perpetual harvest in wooded areas.

Standard equipment on a pig includes a remarkable snout that allows them to effortlessly root through the hardest Georgia clay. Of course this deep-rooted desire to, well, *root*, goes unfulfilled for pigs who are raised on cement in factory farms. Even on smaller pasture-based farms, farmers sometimes adulterate the pig by putting rings in their noses so that they can't root. While this allows pigs to graze pastures without destroying them, it surely leaves the pig wondering why it has such a deep longing that goes unfulfilled. Some farmers go further by trimming needle teeth, docking tails, castrating males, and removing tusks from boar pigs. Each of these actions is designed to better conform the pig to the farmer's needs, with none being for the benefit of the pig.

As we began our farming career we were curious why so much effort was always made to conform animals to mankind's environment rather than adapting farming models to the animals' natural environment and behavior. We understood that doing so made it easier on the farmers, but did it make it right? We didn't think so. Then again, if there was a matter of personal safety then we certainly understood how an animal might need to be adulterated. An example of this may be dehorning milking cows when they're young, as we read stories about people who were killed by the horn of a cow they were milking. You have to draw the line somewhere.

With pigs we hoped to create a safe environment without us modifying them and, most importantly, without them reshaping us! Our goal was to raise animals not only in their natural environment but also to honor and mimic nature to the extent practicable. Nature doesn't castrate pigs or put rings in their noses and neither would we. Neither needs to be done to safely produce delicious and nutritious meat. And so it was with great joy that we watched our first pigs rooting through the woods, digging up whatever they wanted, and just being pigs.

By this time we had added our first boar to the mix, which we had procured from a registered Berkshire breeder in northwest Georgia. To instill confidence in the youngster I named him Pounder and added him to the paddock with Duke and Stub, adjacent to the gilts. Normally the goal is to breed gilts for the first time at about nine months of age so that they will give birth, or farrow, at just past their first birthday. We marked this day on the calendar and when March came I was eager to let the breeding begin. I figured that Pounder would be too.

We had decided to start the breeding with our two largest gilts, Birdie and Dottie. As I walked out to the paddocks to introduce them to Pounder I began recounting what Chris had told me about breeding when he dropped off the pigs. He had told me that sometimes a young boar doesn't really know how to breed at first, and you might need to help him.

"Help him?" I remember asking. "How?"

"Well—by helping him to put it in," he replied.

"How?" I asked, alarmed that he may answer.

"Take it in your hands and put it in for him," he said.

Evidently the man was serious. Or was he? It crossed my mind that this could have been one of those jokes told to city slickers new to country life. Back when I was eighteen years old, on my first "real" work day a production manager sent me on a mission to retrieve some headlamp fluid for him. I was sent from person to person, all of whom were, unlike yours truly, quite aware that headlamps needed no fluid. Perhaps Chris was pulling the wool over my eyes.

"Otherwise, they could lose their confidence and never try again," he explained.

I took him at his word and offered a silent prayer that Pounder descended from the Ron Jeremy of the swine world. As I closed in on the paddock I feared the worst. Here we were, wanting to raise animals naturally. Was it natural that I, a human, helped the boar to—uh—you know, get his mojo on?

Dread overcame me but I resolved to farmer up. I opened the gate to let Birdie and Dottie in, both of which were eager to go. At least *they* seemed to know the drill. Pounder's attention turned to the girls although he showed a slight preference for Dottie who stood for him. When a pig (or cow or ewe, for that matter) is ready to be bred she will stand for her suitor without moving. The moving was left to Pounder who indeed moved into position and, making this papa proud, climbed aboard and got ready for action. I took a ringside seat right on piggy pervert row so that I could be sure to watch the deed happen.

I'll never forget what I saw next.

With Pounder in position to claim his manhood, I saw him begin to uncloak his—*wait*—what the heck is THAT! I couldn't believe what I was seeing as a long, corkscrew-shaped thing emerged from where I figured his privates should have been. Naturally I hastily got out my camera to capture this, thinking for sure that *National Geographic* would relish in my remarkable discovery, although I quickly thought better of it out of fear that they might name it after me! I could just see the TV show now likely narrated by a fearless Australian naturalist who might introduce my discovery to an unsuspecting public in a manner of, "And here is the wild, ferocious boar in the midst of mating season, with his Timmy at the ready as the vicious boar prepares to unleash a new generation of progeny." Great. I would go down in history as the guy who discovered the pig pecker. No thanks.

Instead I called Liz and urged her to run out and see this thing. I had never really wondered where the phrase "screwing" had originated but now I knew for sure. Still stunned by the shock of the sight I watched in a daze as Pounder thrust back and forth with the tip of his corkscrew hitting everything but the target.

Oh no, I said to no one. I'll have to help him.

In rapid succession thoughts of dread crossed my mind. Poor Pounder, I thought. His father was a $20,000 boar, although Pounder himself had been procured for the bargain basement price of $300. Now Pounder couldn't figure out the most basic of biological acts on his own. Have we really gotten our animals this far away from nature where they can't even figure out how to breed? Did he at least know how to go to the bathroom? I donned my latex gloves and got ready to move in.

Just then a miracle of sorts happened as Pounder, flailing his stick at every conceivable target, managed to hit the right one! I paused and watched patiently for a moment. Dottie waited even more patiently, as she must have wondered what the heck was going on back there.

Nothing was going on. That was the problem!

Not recognizing that he had hit pay dirt, Pounder pulled out of the target as quickly as he went in, and continued probing for anything and everything. He stopped for a second. Then as if something clicked in his brain Pounder said, "Wait a minute—what was that a second ago?" His memory steered the probe back until his brain shouted, "STOP! G–O–A–L!"

Pounder liked this. He liked it a lot. Dottie looked as indifferent as before, still wondering what was going on. Pounder went in as far as he could and just stayed there for several minutes. At this point I became a little self-aware that I was watching, and, let's be honest, almost participating in a *ménage à trois* of piggy porn. I turned to look over my shoulder in the woods and then out into the fields to see if there were any witnesses. Relieved to see no one, I waited for the act to be consummated and then waited longer for the next victim, Birdie, to repeat the process.

Fortunately Pounder had figured it out and the second time riding the bike was a breeze.

Liz hadn't arrived at the paddock yet so I went to find her. Over dinner I showed her my illicit pictures of Pounder's privates, which began a disturbing trend of our comfortably discussing testicles at dinner. Later this would evolve to include excrement, animals eating placentas, vaginal prolapses, nasal discharges, compost, and many fundamental biological acts that, in more refined circles, are not fit for the dinner table. Or any conversation.

Yep, our weaning from city life was definitely complete.

We marked the date on the calendar and prepared to wait 114 long days. As we crossed the days off we looked for signs that Dottie would be ready to farrow. We were pleased that the due date was late June, a time when we wouldn't have to worry about cold temperatures. Like Randy said, we were looking for Dottie to bag up and indeed she began to several days before her expected due date. Liz began to fret over our decision to not help Dottie at all with farrowing.

Most farmers help their sows at time of farrowing by providing a farrowing hut, an enclosure in which the sow can retreat to have her young. There's nothing wrong with this and is often done by the farmer out of compassion, both for the comfort of the mother and for the safety of the piglets who may otherwise be inadvertently crushed by the mother. It's also done for economic reasons as it ensures a higher survival rate of piglets. Of course, in nature no one gives a farrowing hut to a sow and she does just fine. Then again, if she's in nature, she's not an industrial breed pig. It was our goal to return animals to a natural setting. Accordingly we had decided to provide no assistance whatsoever, other than ensuring whatever paddock they had provided them the environment in which they could make a nest.

Under a huge oak tree behind our pond, Dottie, perhaps without fully understanding why, began to root and dig a depression in which she could lie. We took this as a sign that she was making a nest, and indeed she took a twig or two there and made what she considered to be, I am sure, a fine nest.

More often than not, sows, cows and ewes give birth during the dark hours, and this was the case with Dottie. As we arrived the next morning there she was with a litter of six little Berkshire piggies! I am not sure how Dottie felt, but we were so proud! They were the cutest little things we had ever seen. Naturally we doted over them for a long time before finally respecting nature and letting Dottie be with her babies. Dottie called to her babies with a deep, guttural grunting sound that she had never uttered before. Later we would witness all sows do this from the minute their babies were born.

We were still in the midst of getting the pastures in shape and I had some bush hogging to do. Between the summer Georgia temperatures and the heat from the tractor engine, mowing was uncomfortable at best. No matter, with a pair of headphones piping in Bob Seger's "Like a Rock," I felt deeply content! Overlooking the pastures from the seat of the tractor filled me with such a sense of connection to the land that just felt so uplifting. I was so happy to be where I was.

As I turned the north end of the farm I looked back to the pond and then to the oak tree where Dottie was sunning, I presumed, with her babies. I squinted, staring into the afternoon sun and finally made out Liz flailing her arms at me. She was standing next to Dottie. I shut off the bush hog, put the tractor into high gear and motored over, and before I even stopped I saw what was bothering Liz.

She was holding a dead piglet.

The journey from exhilaration to utter remorse was instant and is a journey that, unbeknownst to us at the time, we would now perpetually endure. We would never become comfortable with it.

Evidently Dottie had stepped on this young piglet, or rolled on it and crushed it. We were heartbroken. We closely examined Dottie's nest where Liz noticed that one other piglet had a cut on its rear leg. We presumed this was also from being stepped on. As Dottie was lying down in the nest we watched the piglets crawl over one another in an attempt to nurse, never hanging on to a teat for more than a second or two. To make sure that Dottie was producing milk I gently made my way to her nest and squeezed a couple of teats. Yep, milk was flowing and I had now milked a pig. My résumé was becoming more impressive by the second.

Our instincts were to intervene and somehow help the piglets, instantly challenging our values with our first breeding experience. We debated the issue as would become our habit anytime we endured the hardship of watching animals suffer. We decided to trust nature, as cruel as she may be at times. If we intervened to provide support then how would we ever establish a herd of animals that knew how to live a natural life? Surely Dottie would have the instincts to know how to care for her young.

She didn't.

The next morning we awoke to another dead piglet, the one with the cut on its leg. We were disappointed but not surprised. Dottie was lying in the nest with four piglets nursing her and seemed to be doing a good job mothering her young.

She wasn't.

The following morning we were stunned to find only two piglets alive. Two more piglets that looked beautifully healthy the night before now lay dead in and around the nest while

Dottie seemed indifferent. We removed the dead piglets, a task with which we would become all too familiar, and discussed what we should do. Dottie no longer looked bagged up or like she had any milk at all. Liz insisted that I milk her again and this time her suspicions were correct. Dottie had no milk that we could detect. Giving in to her instincts to mother and protect, Liz intervened, removed the two piglets whom we named Daisy and Brutus, and elected to bottle-feed them. We figured that maybe Dottie was too young to mother and didn't "get it," and this would be the only chance these two would have.

We decided we would give Dottie another chance to breed in a few months. When we did she had her second litter just shy of two years old and tirelessly popped out a litter of thirteen! Then we watched in horror as piglet after piglet died until, after seven days, all thirteen piglets were dead. This occurred even though we had set-up an electric fence paddock within a paddock in a last-ditch effort to help Dottie save herself, forcing her to stay with her young and away from other sows. Dottie, despite our love for her, just had no maternal instincts and there was no room on our farm for animals that didn't pull their weight.

She had to go.

The prior summer, just after Dottie had her first litter, the other five Berkshire sows each farrowed, giving birth to about forty-five piglets total in June and July. On one particular day three young sows all gave birth, evidently in the middle of the night before. I remember going into the paddock to check on them in the July heat only to be greeted first by swarming flies. A string of dead piglets were strewn everywhere, a sight so vivid and surreal that it seemed impossible to believe. Of the twenty-eight piglets that were born that day, twenty died quickly or before I arrived, being completely abandoned and unattended by their mothers. The lone exception was Birdie, who demonstrated good mothering skills, keeping alive six of the seven she gave birth to.

Confused and unsure of ourselves, we were completely torn about what to do and began to question our values right out of the gate. We knew that we could have intervened with farrowing huts and perhaps saved the lives of many of the piglets. When you love animals you can't stand to see them suffer, and we love animals. We debated and challenged each other's thinking, and I know that Liz wanted to intervene many times and give the pigs some help. All we wanted was for the pigs to rejoice in living a natural life but they just didn't know how. These instincts had been bred out of them over generations, a realization that we would soon discover with virtually every species we were to raise on our farm. It killed me to not help the piglets, but, as I pointed out to Liz, if we started propping up the animals with support now, when would we ever stop? When would they ever learn and adapt?

No, as hard as it was to endure it seemed clear to me that we had to prioritize the health and vigor of the species and the herd over the individual. And that meant breeding resistance to diseases and parasites and breeding in strong maternal instincts. We would try again with each of these sows, only to learn just as hard a lesson the second and third time around that these Berkshire sows just weren't capable of being good mothers in our very natural setting.

By the end of our third year, Pounder and the Berkshire sows would be gone from our farm.

The Ossabaw Island breed of pigs, on the other hand, proved to be fantastic mothers and foragers. Only one generation removed from the wild, our Ossabaws demonstrated great skill at making nests and keeping their piglets alive. Time after time, when a sow was ready to farrow, she would begin ripping up privet, yellow crownbeard or whatever was in her area to build a large, rounded nest. The other sows would help her, demonstrating a strong sense of social bonding when one of their tribe was about to give birth. The mother-to-be would crawl into her nest, give birth to her young, and not emerge, as far as we could tell, for a few days. When she did, an average of five or six fat round little piglets would be in close pursuit. Finding a dead Ossabaw piglet would prove to be, thankfully, an extremely rare sighting.

Pigs were a good first species for us to start with. We learned from them that, while we may be rookies at farming, industrial breed animals are, astonishingly, rookies at knowing how to truly live in the natural settings from which they evolved. We had to learn to farm naturally alongside animals that had to learn to live naturally. We clearly needed to carefully select breeds and genetics who could thrive in the environment we were hoping to champion on their behalf. Our experiences with pigs forced us to think long and hard about the farming model we were pursuing. How could we restore the instincts that factory farming had suppressed without letting them root, wallow and destroy our land?

Pigs also challenged us to think carefully about how we tended the land. When we first gazed upon the neglected fields of Nature's Harmony Farm we were unable to really appreciate how much forested land we had. We later learned that, of the original seventy-two acres, at least twenty acres were wooded. Today that number is about double since our farm now encompasses one hundred twenty-six acres. Typically if your aim is to farm you hope to see open land that can be used either for grazing, vegetable or fruit production. So what's the most natural, productive way to use the woodlot? Woodlot pork made perfect sense to us, and we rigged paddocks of portable electric fencing in and around the trees to give our piggies large paddocks to roam. We would move these paddocks approximately every month so that the ground wasn't torn up or compacted too badly.

The pigs were thrilled to be in the woods of course and were able to forage for much, but not all, of their food. To forage for all of their food a farmer would have to think more along the lines of acres per pig versus pigs per acre. We wanted to mimic nature within an agricultural context but in the end our aim was to produce clean, safe, delicious food from animals that enjoyed life. Their food would need to be supplemented in one way or another. The only question was how.

Large breeds such as Berkshires also have, not surprisingly, large hooves. This combined with their prodigious frames, means that they are hard on the land. They can dig enormous wallows and trample the land so that it becomes as hard as concrete. By contrast, the diminutive Ossabaw Island hog has dainty feet and legs. More nimble and agile, they are nowhere near as hard on the land and indeed resemble a more natural pig that you would see in the wild than a factory-farmed breed. Almost by definition, they can feed themselves, as they have been doing for hundreds of years since the last wave of Spaniards stranded them on the island off the Georgia coast. They too would require some supplemental feed since we were limiting the area they could roam but they would be much easier to handle in that regard.

When we first contemplated raising Ossabaws after visiting a farmer in North Carolina, we were warned that they would be too difficult a breed to start with and we were encouraged to pursue "friendlier" breeds. Ironically, from the first time we had Ossabaws on our farm we've been able to walk up to the girls anytime to pet, scratch and bond with them. We run our fingers through their long, wiry hair and thoroughly enjoy their company. They indeed are a breed to be honored and respected.

The boys, however, tended to walk on the wild side. When they are young they are just as easy to handle as the girls are. As they mature, in part because we don't castrate them, they begin to look and act more like wild boars. Actually the boar's behavior has an interesting dichotomy to it. On the one hand they are quick to scurry off into the woods if we're walking by, or if they feel challenged they will open their mouth and oscillate their lower jaw, exhibiting to us their razor sharp tusks. Then they take their front feet and paw the ground, a sure find that they are prepared to accept our invitation to battle. Yet other times they run up like friendly puppies that can't wait to see us. If we're driving the ATV or tractor out to visit they respond to that sound by rushing to the fence to greet us, and indeed we get in with them and commingle. They don't like to be scratched and groomed as much as the girls do, but like the teenager who so fiercely wants his independence, they still cling to the company of mom and dad, personified in this case by farmer Tim and farmer Liz.

For us it was the rare breed pigs that we grew to love and that worked the best on our farm. We later added Large Black pigs, an old breed with large, floppy ears that cover their eyes, making it difficult for them to see. As a result they lumber slowly around the farm. We affectionately refer to them as the "floppies."

Both the Ossabaws and Large Blacks do a commendable job of helping to keep invasive plants such as Chinese privet and yellow crownbeard in the woods and out of the pastures. And so we found that our acres and acres of woodlands could be just as productive as our pastures. It proved to be such a perfect habitat for pigs that it made us really wonder why everyone doesn't raise pigs in their woods. Strangely, woodlots often go unused by farmers, yet raising pigs is an easy way to make the land productive. There's plenty of forage that pigs will gladly harvest themselves, although unless they are stocked at much lower densities than what would be profitable in an agricultural setting, they need some supplemental feed.

We devised an approach to supplement their feed partially with whey, which will be discussed in a later chapter, and by planting crops for them to joyously harvest on their own. From turnips to peas to sweet potatoes and pumpkins our approach would be to define paddocks months in advance of moving in the pigs, and plant crops adjacent to their woodlot paddock. This method allows them to not only harvest their own feed but also use their remarkable snout to plow up our field and deposit fertilizer simultaneously, rendering it ready for the next crop. All without a drop of diesel fuel being used. They would return to this paddock months later to harvest a different crop, not only working for a living on this farm, but relishing every moment of it. If this all sounds a bit old-fashioned, it is. And that's the idea. In the farming model we envisaged, pigs would be living the life a pig was meant to live and neither they nor we would have it any other way. Some people view our farming model as ultra modern, others view it as obsolete. I view it as sensible.

With the woodlots now being utilized not only productively but also in a manner that gave animals real pleasure, our attention turned to our vast and worn-out fields. Fields that echoed mournful dirges for the health they once had and the health they so desperately longed to enjoy once again.

CROP FAILURE

BY LIZ YOUNG

From a Nature's Harmony Farm Blog Post, July 10, 2008

I've never thought about what this could really mean to a farmer. Last year, when northern Georgia had an unusually late freeze around Easter, the news had story after story about farmers who were looking at 80-100% crop failures on peaches, pecans, blueberries, and apples. They showed videos of dead frost-bitten tree limbs being sawed off and burned. Of course I thought it must be devastating to those poor farmers, but when the story was over the thoughts left my mind.

Well, Tim and I are amidst a total crop failure and I am all too close to a reality that no one should ever have to bear. We farm livestock, not plants, but the concept is the same. We procure or produce young animals like a crop farmer buys or saves seeds. We give them everything they need to grow big and strong—tending to them each day and always worrying about their health, just like a crop farmer would for their plants. For all of us, the end result is food and our payment comes from selling that food. It's this payment that allows us to live and to continue to farm the next crop.

Well, what happens when something goes terribly wrong? When that crop which you were depending on fails? It's like heading into work one day to find out that your company has closed. The future that you were depending on is no longer there. There will be no paycheck.

We have made many investments on the farm and one is an investment in animals. People often ask us what it takes to get into farming the way we have and one thing that is often overlooked is the price of the animals. The animals are your paycheck. Pure breeds will cost top dollar. For breeding stock, we have bought six Berkshire gilts and one Berkshire boar. We also bought four Ossabaw gilts and one Ossabaw boar. We have been waiting months for them to breed and the next step in the plan is finally here. We had six successful breedings with the Berkshires—all have been obviously pregnant for over a month now.

The Ossabaws are much harder to tell. Their bodies don't take on the same shape and their udders don't "belly down" or fill up with milk in such an obvious manner so we have had trouble telling if they are bred or not. These expected piglets are our crop and our livelihood. We are already lining up customers who would be interested in buying pork at the end of this year. We were expecting around sixty hogs to be ready in December and January. That's a *lot* of food!

Well, all of our Berkshires have finished farrowing and the result has been *twelve* live piglets. Not sixty, not even thirty. At the current time there are just twelve. That's like eighty-percent crop failure. And it is still very early. Some piglets are less than a week old. There could be more casualties along the way. What is the reality of this? Remember that passing thought of showing up to work one day and the company has closed? That's the reality.

What a horrible week last week was. We had two Berkshires who looked ready to deliver. On Thursday when we went to check on them we walked up on dead piglets in the woods. They were scattered about everywhere. Some live piglets were running around as well, but we didn't see any mothers laying down or attending to their piglets. We didn't even know who belonged to whom. We have put the puzzle pieces together as best we can and figure that three Berkshires delivered all at the same time early that morning. One seemed to have delivered prematurely—all of her piglets were too weak to survive. The other two seemed to have a few successful live births, but neither had mothering instincts. They kept walking away from the babies and had not even built a nest. We took all of the piglets to try to raise ourselves.

Later that afternoon we found Ossabaw piglets in their paddock and the same thing—no mother to claim them! To this day we're not even sure who the mother was. There were three live piglets that we took from there giving us ten piglets to bottle-feed from four sows. We spent days trying to nurse these weak piglets attending to feedings every hour, but by Sunday there were no survivors.

Since then, the last Berkshire has delivered and did the same thing. She was walking away from her young and would not lie down to let them nurse. We penned her up with them to force the bond. Now four are alive and apparently doing well.

What went wrong? In our opinion, it was young inexperienced mothers. For starters, I believe they were bred too young. The breeders that we got them from told us they could breed at five months. I think that giving them some more time to mature would have been better. It's like a thirteen-year-old having a baby, panicking, and not knowing what to do with them. These were also all first-time mothers—things were bound to be difficult. However, we have confidence that our pigs can be great mothers in time. One older Berkshire (Birdie) has done a fabulous job! We will give them all another chance to breed and hope for another "crop" in the future.

The realities of crop failure can be devastating and it's not something that you recover from by the time the news story has ended. We will carry the burden until the next crop begins to flourish. This means trying to save as many of the living piglets as we can so that we can have some pork to sell this winter. Even into this fall we will be remembering this failure as we explain to customers that we have a limited amount of food for them. But luckily for us, a pig's gestation cycle is short—less than four months—so once they begin to breed again, we can be optimistic for more piglets in the pretty near future.

CHAPTER 6

Reviving the Prairie

March 2008 arrived with a vengeance. I awoke one morning to dense fog, driving rain and near-freezing temperatures as I cranked my truck at 3:00 a.m., beginning a nineteen-hour roundtrip to pick up an Ossabaw Island boar at George Washington's birthplace in Virginia.

The month of March was a milestone for us as farmers, something of a perfect storm. Here I was rushing off in the fog of night to get our first Ossabaw boar on the same day that we were set to receive our first order of baby chicks, some four hundred newly hatched broilers that would arrive at the post office in a few hours for Liz to tend to. Since neither of us had ever even held a baby chick, she was nervous, but I reassured her they would be comfortable in the new brood house the two of us had just built.

Perhaps she was nervous because it wasn't only the chicks she had to attend to in my absence. We had begun raising cows a few months before, arriving about the same time as our

Berkshire pigs. For the first two months the cows remained in a large paddock where we fed them hay but with spring approaching they were now being rotationally grazed and moved to fresh pasture each day. Liz would have to set up a paddock and move the cows during my absence as well.

After careful deliberation we had selected the Murray Grey breed of cows as the foundation of our herd. Not widely known in the United States, Murray Greys began in Australia along the Murray River in New South Wales. Over time, Murray Greys began to win carcass competitions and developed an impressive reputation for easy fleshing and high quality beef. They have grey or black skin color to protect against cancer eye and sunburned udders, and their silver reflects the sun allowing them to withstand extreme heat, which is important in our Georgia summers. The Murray Grey cow is known for her outstanding maternal characteristics and high production of milk for her calves. Add to all of this their reputation for docility and calving ease and it was easy for Liz and I to settle on this breed. In our oppressive summer heat we couldn't figure for the life of us why so many farmers preferred black cattle.

We had purchased a number of heifer calves along with several cows that had been bred by the prior owners in Ohio and Oklahoma. We figured soon enough we would find out how easily they calved and how good of mothers they would make, but we weren't prepared to deal with that yet. That didn't matter.

My phone rang when I was about an hour over the Virginia line. It was Liz, who by this time had picked up the chicks from the post office and settled them into their toasty new brood house.

"The wind and rain is coming inside the brood house," she cried. "It's blowing snow here and fifteen chicks are already dead!"

I didn't know what to say or how to react. Battling the high gusts and staying focused on the road while also trying to figure out what to do when I was hours away, I just tried to comfort Liz.

"We don't even know what normal is," I said. "Maybe it's normal for fifteen chicks out of four hundred to not make it their first day, we don't know."

"They're shivering," was all she could muster, and through her tears she explained how she was putting up tarps to try and shield where the wind and rain was coming in.

When we built the brood house we left a four-inch opening along the top for ventilation. We had read that drafts needed to be avoided but ventilation was important. Regardless, this brood house was battling nature and nature was winning easily. In response, Liz put up makeshift tarps, adjusted heat lamps and did what she could to make the chicks comfortable. I felt awful being that far away, but still had another twelve hours at least before I would see her.

It was just past noon when I pulled into the George Washington's birthplace monument in Westmoreland County, Virginia. At present the monument tries to preserve and recreate the scene to mirror how it likely was in Washington's time. This includes having livestock and, in particular, pens that housed Ossabaw Island hogs, the breed that would have most resembled pigs of Washington's day. I stepped out into a cold steady rain and was taken to a very muddy hog paddock that was enclosed by a split-rail fence. I scanned the area for a place that animals could be loaded or unloaded, to no avail. There was only a pen.

A guide arrived and showed me the young piglets, explaining that I could take my preference for the agreed upon price of \$40. It was this price and the fact that a young boar was available that inspired my trek to Virginia. The guide appeared to be in his mid-fifties, and his physical appearance suggested many years spent behind a desk.

"How do you want to load him?" I inquired, nervously anticipating his reply.

Silence. There was no plan. Finally, he offered, "Let's get in and see if we can pin him up."

The smell of the pig muck that I then stepped deeply into would now be my companion all the way home, as I did not have a change of clothes or shoes. I had expected to load up a pig and be on my way quickly, but clearly that was wishful thinking.

The ordeal took ninety minutes and made for your typical Keystone Cops comic reel of two tall guys each with only two legs chasing a low-to-the-ground four-legged beast who could easily out maneuver us in the muck. And did. With one of us using feed as lure while the other pushed a board behind we finally pinned the boar against some boards so that he was trapped.

"Great!" I exclaimed. "Now what?"

Again, silence.

"How should we get him to the truck?" I continued.

More silence. Clearly I was the farmer, even though I had yet to fully embrace the transition from urban life. Oh well, time to farmer up. I asked him to hold the pig in place as I pulled my truck immediately alongside the split-rail fence, which was about five feet tall. I returned to the paddock and got my hands around the forty-pound boar, lifting him up closely to my chest. Now, forty pounds isn't really that much for me to lift. But a scared, muddy forty-pound boar with four legs flailing, kicking and pushing off of me was like trying to hold an armful of greased bowling balls. It was all I could do to hold on but the worst wasn't over. With no door or gate for me to use I literally had to climb up the split-rail fence with the pig and put him into the back of my truck. I then had to quickly jump over and put the top over the pickup bed so that the boar didn't jump out! All of which I did, to my own astonishment!

As the guide came over and I prepared to pay him he said, "Keep it, no charge." He continued, out of breath, "You earned it."

And so we had our first Ossabaw boar, which I quickly named Charlie Brown in honor of the orange/black striped pattern that resembled Charlie Brown's shirt. I began the long trip home and wanted to call Liz, but I was out of range. I must have come into range about forty-five minutes later, because the phone rang and it was Liz.

"Dixie just had her calf and I don't know what to do!" was the greeting I heard when I answered.

"What?," I replied, "She's not due until—"

"Tell that to Dixie," interrupted Liz. "The calf is on the ground, but it's blowing snow here and she's freezing!" she quivered. "And the chicks are freezing too! When will you be home"?

"Not until at least eight or nine o'clock tonight," I said. "I'll call Randy."

Dixie, one of the Murray Grey cows we purchased from Oklahoma, had just had her first calf. Clearly Liz wasn't ready for all this. It was too much to ask of anyone new to farming to deal with cows, pigs, new calves, four hundred baby chicks, and horrific weather on their own. To make it worse, we still had no house on the land, so Liz had no protection from the weather herself other than to seek refuge in the brood house. I called Randy and pleaded if he could go over and offer Liz some assistance. Looking back, I have no idea if he was at home or at work or where. No matter, he went and, according to Liz just stared at the calf and its momma.

"Well, that's what cows do. They have calves," he told her.

"But she'll freeze," Liz explained.

"Ah, she won't freeze," Randy stated confidently in the kind of southern, country drawl that makes it very difficult to determine where one word ends and the next begins. "Her momma will take care of her."

And I guess that was that.

When I got home that night the calf, which Randy and Liz had named Delight, was indeed fine. This began a tradition on our farm of whoever finds the calf names the calf, as long as the newborn's name begins with the same letter that begins her mother's name. And so Dixie had Delight, the next year she would have Daphne and two years later Delight's first calf would be named Dandi, continuing the string of female calves from that line. The entire family lives happily together in the herd today, so clearly Delight was OK just as Randy had said.

Liz, on the other hand, wasn't OK. Since that day we've had a lot of ups and downs on the farm, but I honestly believe this was the worst day of our farming life for Liz. I thought there was better than a fifty-percent chance she'd want to throw in the towel after that. I know she contemplated it. We just weren't ready for everything that hit us at once and she can't stand not being fully prepared. It wasn't her fault. It was mine, as I had pushed us too hard and too fast to get everything up and running, even before we lived on the land. Regardless, we couldn't stop now. We already had over a dozen cows, pregnant sows and now almost four hundred chicks that depended on us. We started sprinting to catch up and kept running for the next three years.

When we first contemplated moving to the country we didn't figure that we would end up raising a bunch of cows. Or sheep, and hundreds of laying hens, for that matter. And we weren't inspired to do so as a result of the burgeoning market demand for grass-fed meats and free-range eggs. As I walked our crunchy, rocky, neglected fields, they cried to me and I heard their plea for help. After years and years of neglect they needed healing. But what could we do?

Seeking wisdom I tirelessly turned weathered pages in search of inspiration from yesterday's sages. Perhaps the author that inspired me the most in my search for answers was Sir Albert Howard. His writings, set down some sixty-odd years earlier, made a sensible case that all health is connected and emanates from the soil. The health of the soil nourishes the forages that it produces which in turn nourishes the eater, which in turn, if you're a carnivore, nourishes you.

Clever farmers can come up with some pretty catchy ways of describing what all this means, such as grass farming, carbon sequestering, solar capturing and so on. But the reality is that any conscientious and sustainable farming model has to begin with a profound respect for the soil and an absolute commitment to building and protecting it.

For our part we never contemplated farming the land any other way than organically. This wasn't driven by marketing or customer demand, as, in the beginning, we weren't seeking customers or even to be a farm. Rather we were just trying to take a piece of land, steward it for the rest of our lives, and leave it far better off than we found it. Dousing the land with chemical fertilizers, herbicides and pesticides never made sense to us. Those are the tools of those who chase yield and maximum productivity, but that was never our aim.

Weren't the land and the prairies healthy before man, the machine and chemicals intervened? How did these ecosystems thrive before they succumbed to cultivation and urban development? The answer, I believe, was interdependent balance.

The prairies were historically characterized by rich diversity of animal species attracted to, and dependent on, the rich diversity of forage species. As grasses grew and dried in hot conditions, fire emerged as an essential ingredient in maintaining the balance of the ecosystem. Otherwise large oak and hickory trees would have grown to claim a dominating position in the quest to harvest sunlight. After fires, young lush grasses emerged, attracting and depending on grazers—in ancient times they were mammoths, camels and mastodons, and more recently, bison. Bison populations grew in astonishing numbers, reaching an estimated sixty to seventy million and dividing into herds that, in the mid-1800s, would take horseback riders several days to cross.[7]

Grazers such as bison evolved to consume enormous amounts of high-fiber, low-protein forages. Constantly moving, grazing, trampling and fertilizing, the bison held grass (and tree) growth in check, creating prodigious amounts of biomass and rich topsoil. These herbivores attracted other animal species, including over four hundred bird species. The habits of the herbivores created an irresistible environment for the birds that were drawn to the countless leafhoppers, grasshoppers and other insects that were stirred up as the bison trampled and voraciously ingested the grasses. The birds such as brown cowbirds and Brewer's blackbirds, and grouse such as the greater prairie chicken also relished the insect larvae and dung beetles that were incubating in fresh bison dung. The relationship became symbiotic as birds depended on, and benefited from, the bison, and indeed perched atop them. This way they could dig their feet into a warm, furry blanket when winter temperatures necessitated it. In turn the birds were assigned to constant guard duty, with their fluttering alerting the bison to danger that may otherwise have gone unnoticed.

Interesting, but how does all of this history of grazing prairies apply to us as farmers today? The prairie model that evolved naturally worked beautifully, sustaining abundant populations of healthy bison and countless other animals while enriching the soil. Could we as regular people—not necessarily biologists or ranchers—endeavor to truly recreate, or mimic, this model? We would attempt to. Our aim was to mimic nature and revive the prairie within an agricultural setting.

We approached establishing such an environment in a number of concurrent rather than sequential ways, which, upon reflection, is why our farm grew so quickly. Effectively, nature decreed it. We needed to rebuild organic matter that would support lush forage growth but at the same time we needed grazers to graze what forages we did have and distribute fertilizer that would provide the organic matter we sought. How could we do one without the other?

Sensing that this was a chicken-and-egg question, the natural answer was to simultaneously add chickens to the mix to emulate the role of the prairie birds. This act was to be performed by the chicks of the laying hen variety we had just placed in the brood house. They would join fifty or so other mature laying hens we had already purchased that would collectively domicile in an eggmobile, one of two I had built over the winter from abandoned cotton wagons. By midsummer we would have three hundred laying hens roaming the pasture freely, eating grasses, hunting insects, and perhaps most important, scratching through cow patties in search of those tasty grubs. The fact that they laid the best tasting, most nutritious eggs with deep orange yolks and firm whites was a most welcomed fringe benefit.

Usually it's difficult to identify any one particular chicken out of a sea of hundreds of the same breed, but one individual stepped forward to become my favorite.

At this time we still didn't have a home on the farm and were driving back and forth each day to tend to our growing population of critters. One day while I was at the farm and Liz was back home I was strolling the pastures and talking with her on the phone, describing the scene of the chickens ranging behind the cows. One Rhode Island Red chicken kept leaving the others behind to follow me around. Upon noticing this I zigzagged and walked further away to see if it was my imagination. It wasn't. I bent down and she walked right up to me so that I could pick her up.

"Honey, this red chicken keeps following me around," I told Liz.

"What? What does she want?" Liz asked.

How did I know what she wanted? I had never touched a chicken until a month before. It seemed strange to me that she'd prefer to wander with me than to be with her kind, but here she was. I decided to name her Penny since she reminded me of a little red penny that kept showing up. I figured this whole thing was a fluke anyway and that after I released her I'd never recognize her again. But I did. Every time I went out, she'd seek me out. Liz couldn't believe it when she saw it. Frail little Penny looked like an old Granny even though she wasn't old at all, and from then on we always sought her out and never failed to recognize her.

So it was, after closing on the property in January 2007 and fixing up the land all of that year, we began farming in March the following year with pigs in the woods and cows on pasture, followed by laying hens and meat chickens in a separate pasture in chicken tractors. And we still weren't living on the farm yet as our house was a month away from being ready!

We didn't feel good about using the chicken tractor design we saw at the Georgia Organics field day so we designed them in the shape of hoops to see if we could live with that. This provided enough head room for adults to walk into and allowed us to put roosting bars in them. However, we would abandon the practice of confining chickens to the tractors after only one year, opting instead to allow all birds to free-range.

We had now started down the path of mimicking parts of the prairie model with grazers and birds, but where were the predators? The effect of the predators on the prairie was to keep the herd both mobbed up in large numbers for protection and constantly on the move in search of lush forage. We would have to somehow inspire this mob, mow and move behavior, but how? What would be our predators and how would we limit access to only lush, succulent forage?

Most farmers who raise cattle (or horses, for that matter) practice a method called continuous grazing. That is to say, the grazers are allowed to roam freely within the boundaries of the farm, picking whatever they want to eat and whenever they want to eat it. If you're driving through the countryside it's easy to identify farms that practice this method of grazing management by simply looking at the land. I notice three visual clues that instantly jump out.

The first clue is that there are mounds of grass all around the farm. It seems curious to me that with cows on pasture there would be large clumps of untouched grass reaching waist high. Why hadn't the clumps been grazed? The answer is because these clumps marked the spots where cows had defecated earlier, perhaps months earlier. While cows will freely graze around horse or sheep dung, they long ago learned, without any help from humans, that harmful parasites reside in their own dung, so they absolutely refuse to graze in the vicinity as long as they can detect its presence. Most parasites are species-specific, so horse parasites don't bother cows, cow parasites are no threat to sheep, and so on. Interestingly, if you were to simply cut the tall grass emanating from the cow dung and lay it elsewhere in the pasture, the cow would gladly eat it.[8]

So it's the smell on the ground rather than something to do with the grass that causes this repulsion.

A second clue is that much of the pasture appears to be over-grazed, or eaten to the bare ground. This should come as no surprise since cows have favorite foods just as humans do. A cow grazes by wrapping her sandpaper-like tongue around a plant and ripping it from the ground. Grass plants have a root structure below ground that, in weight, approximates the forage above ground. When a cow takes a bite of one of her favorite forages, such as clover, the plant sheds an amount of root matter that roughly corresponds to the forage ripped by the cow. The root matter that is shed will in time become humus and will add to the soil's organic matter. If there is a non-desirable plant next to the clover, such as pigweed for instance, the cow will pass this up. This allows the pigweed to continue growing, hogging sunlight and shading out the clover, which becomes stunted. A week or so later when the clover has managed to put forth a little more growth, the cow, having no restraints, is free to come and take another bite of her favorite snack. I refer to this as the death bite, as the plant now sheds a dangerous amount of its roots. With its forage now completely eviscerated from above and with no remaining leaf material to harvest solar energy, the area is overgrazed and outmatched by the undesirable plants, known to us humans as weeds. Regrettably, this paradigm doesn't apply to humans. Otherwise we would have long ago overgrazed Big Macs, pizzas and chips, and we would be stuck with weedy broccoli, okra, Swiss chard and grapes, creating an environment in which we apparently could not survive. Evidently we can continue producing an abundant, unending supply of our favorite foods—or so we believe.

Which brings me to the third clue, which reveals itself as patches of tall weeds in the pasture. A sure sign of a continuously grazed pasture is one where clumps of beautiful but untouched grass are present next to large areas of tightly grazed areas, with unsightly weeds of all varieties interspersed between the two. In our area these weeds are most commonly pigweed, thistle, dog fennel, pokeweed and the like. Not able to graze the clumps of lush forage near their dung and refusing to graze weeds that may be poisonous to them, such as pokeweed, the cows must persistently nibble dangerously close to the ground where they are quite likely to ingest the parasites that tend to linger on the bottom two or three inches of a grass plant. Parasite control is manageable via chemicals to farmers who are so inclined but it is costly and definitely not natural. Since we were focused on mimicking nature, we would need to control parasites naturally.

The solution to all of these dilemmas can be found in the concept of management-intensive grazing (MIG). In contrast to continuous grazing, MIG is a system that employs electric fencing and temporary posts configured into small paddocks, roughly the size of one day's worth of grazing. To set it up you simply walk along a line, push a step-in post into the ground, take a reel of electric twine to roll out a fence before finally connecting an energizer, or charger, to the fence. In terms of mimicking nature the electric fence actually plays the role of the wolf, or predator, by keeping the cows mobbed up in place. With nowhere to go and nothing to eat but what's right in front of them, the cows begin to mob graze.

Cows don't eat standing still. Rather they constantly move around the paddock in circles, following their instincts to move ahead for food even though lush grass may be a foot or two to their side. Their natural instincts to move ahead is what always kept them safe from parasites. Mow, move and leave the parasites behind in the form of fertilizer.

Our goal with MIG is for them to eat sixty percent of the paddock, trample twenty percent, and leave the rest. We figured they would first eat their favorite forages such as clover, so the goal with trampling is for them to trample weeds or undesirable plants, working as much organic matter as they can into the soil. If the paddock is sized too small they're likely to bite a particular plant twice, resulting in the plant shedding a dangerous amount of its root mass and energy reserves. After a day of grazing another paddock is set up contiguous to the first, a gate is opened and the cows are moved in. Actually, "moved in" is a bit of a misnomer. A more accurate description would be that *we* move out of the way. The cows, out of lush forage but able to see and salivate over what's in the next paddock, are as eager to move as you are to move them. Simply open the gate, smile, step aside and watch them devour the lush forage. Sounds simple enough, but as with everything we did, it wasn't simple to move the cows the first time we tried.

When we received the cows in the winter, we penned them up in an area of pasture that would later become our garden. For two months we fed the cows hay while they enriched the soil for a garden we would plant a year later. When it came time move the cows onto fresh pasture we assumed we would just string a paddock and march the cows in. The problem of course is that this system of MIG was new to both us *and* the cows. We ran an electric fence chute to the new paddock; I got in and walked ahead of the cows and, like an idiot, called to them like I was calling a puppy. "Here cows!" I kept calling and walking and the cows kept standing, staring and, I suspect saying silently to one another, "How'd we get stuck with this farmer?"

The cows didn't budge. Back then I think I called Randy half a dozen times a day. I am surprised he didn't change his number. I placed another call and he motored over, this time with his five-year-old son, Slayter. I told him what I was trying to do and before I could finish the sentence, Slayter jumped in the paddock over the electric fence, got behind the cows and started yelling, "Go on girls, go on now!" The cows obeyed and Slayter drove them into the new paddock, an event we immortalized for Slayter on our YouTube channel where he can be heard calling in the background. Now that I had this new technique of attacking the cows from behind rather than luring them from the front, I figured for sure I was headed for farmer

fame. All thanks to a five-year-old. Later I would rea
Temple Grandin and others who would help me become quite
comfortable with how all species on our farm think and react
to my actions, but I sure started out without a clue.

In addition to moving the cows daily there are two additional requirements that must be respected if MIG is to work
well for the land and the grazer. One is to ensure the new paddock is lush and not too overgrown or lignified. The second is
to ensure that the grazers can't return to the paddock they just
grazed until it has entered a period of lush growth, as Voisin
described in *Grass Productivity*. What Voisin found was that the
productivity of the grass could be increased remarkably by
introducing the grazing animal to it at just the right time and
removing it at the appropriate time. MIG evolved as a system
of doing just that.

The goal of orchestrating this intricate dance between
cows, chickens and pigs is to mimic nature's model so that a
rich, nourishing biomass would result. Since we never even
planned to have any in the first place, what would become of
all these cows that we were enlisting to heal the land?

Cows come in two flavors, dairy and beef. As a farmer you
either employ them for milk or you grow and harvest them as
beef. We planned to build a grass-fed beef herd, which definitely bridged the gap between our values of allowing cows to
consume only forage and the consumer demand for grass-fed
beef, which appeared sure to continue rising. There's a problem,
however, and that is that most cows have been bred and selected
for over half a century to finish on grain.

"Finish" is a term that is used to describe when a cow or
steer has fleshed out and is ready for slaughter. Ideally the animal will have reached its genetic potential and for a lengthy

period leading up to the slaughter date will be gaining weight at the rate of about three pounds a day. This results in the beef being well marbled, meeting the tenderness requirements of the demanding American consumer. This remarkable weight gain is usually made possible by thirty-two pounds or so of high-energy grain ration and antibiotics consumed daily by each cow in the feedlot. Equally remarkable is the highly mechanized, diesel-laden process required to grow, harvest and transport all that grain from far and wide to a few massive CAFOs.

So what happens when you put the genetics of a grazing animal that has been bred for a high-energy corn ration on pasture alone? They won't finish. Sure, you can process them, but you'll find the ribeyes won't be well marbled and will be tougher than consumers expect, desire and demand. In my opinion meat from a grazing animal is far healthier than grain-finished meat, but that's not enough to assuage a demanding public. And I don't blame them. We may not be entitled to it, but why shouldn't we desire both nutritious *and* delicious food? The two don't have to be mutually exclusive of one another.

If we hoped to one day offer grass-fed beef that wasn't only nutritious but also tender and delicious, we would have to take a long view and carefully develop those genetics over many years. This is what led us to pursue the Murray Grey breed, a breed that has traditionally been raised on forage alone in areas prone to drought, much like ours. Still, some of the cows we started with were bred for show conditions and these animals had been fed some grain prior to coming to our farm in order to make them "look better." Those days were now behind them. We began what we figured would be at least a ten-year process of breeding, selecting and developing outstanding grass-fed genetics not only for the southeastern United States in general, but for our environment in particular.

There would be no shortcuts here, and realizing this, in a way, put me at ease. Corporate life was all about better, faster, cheaper and instant gratification. In business, there was always a way to win out and beat the competition and the clock. Not so when you're farming naturally. The cows helped me to learn that nature doesn't conform to those human desires and follows its own eternal clock. And so I began to conform myself, with reluctant gratitude, to her pace.

Regardless of what the cows were fed or how they were treated before they made their way to Nature's Harmony Farm, they adapted to our system remarkably quickly. Of course we had countless episodes in the early days of cows getting out, us chasing them around the farm and herding them back in, but, overall, the system of MIG worked smoothly all along.

Until we added the sheep.

Like cows, sheep are ruminants and can thrive on natural forage, eliminating any need for purchased feed. Indeed for millennia sheep have thrived on forage alone, well before the advancement of modern agriculture. When people buy feed for sheep it's either because they don't have pasture or because, for whatever reason, they want to bring feed to the sheep, perhaps for the pleasure of hand feeding them. Our farming model mandated that everyone carry their own weight and that meant that sheep, along with cows, were expected to harvest their own feed and fertilize the land to boot.

Typically sheep prefer legumes and broad-leaf forage to pure pasture. They are apt to browse weeds that are difficult to control otherwise. Thus if grazed alongside cows their dining preferences complement each other, resulting in more evenly grazed paddocks. Later we would add a couple of donkeys to the mix and watch with glee as they grazed young thistle and horse nettle plants.

The challenge with sheep is keeping them in with the cows. To accomplish this objective some farmers use electrified netting which generally comes in rolls approximately 160 feet long and with step-in posts built right into the netting. It's more expensive than just using step-in posts and reels of electric twine, not to mention more cumbersome to set-up and move, but it could work for both cows and sheep if you connected enough rolls. That is, if you could get the posts into the ground. Like all clay-based soils, our soil is very dense. When it came time to build our house we couldn't pass a perk test *anywhere* on our seventy-two-acre spread. That is until I relayed this information to the realtor, who promptly rounded up a seventy-five-year-old soil czar who came out, took the samples and cleared us (barely) to build. Ah, the power of connections!

Septic systems aside, the density and composition of our soil causes it to vacillate between two extremes. When it rains more than a half-inch at a time, a thick, gooey mud forms, making it a challenge to even to walk. The muck grabs your boots with a hold that leaves your foot naked as you unsuspectingly plant your next step.

But when the soil is dry, nothing, and I mean *nothing*, can easily penetrate it.

To illustrate this, consider what we went through to install the 12,000 feet of woven-wire fence around our property. We had the misfortune of beginning our farming career during one of the worst droughts in recent memory in Georgia. Metal T-posts had to be driven into the ground every ten feet or so around the farm to support the fence. Pounding them by hand was possible but extremely exhausting. To ease the pain we would start the posts by hand and then I would slowly lower the bucket of our tractor on top of the post with the aim to hydraulically drive it into the ground. Time after time I watched in disbelief as each T-Post, rather than penetrate our soil, opted to bend in half like a sad, wilted plant. In the end we drove them by hand.

So there was no way the fragile step-in posts embedded in the poultry netting were going into our unyielding ground. The videos on the distributor's website made it look easy, just like the infomercials for those small tillers till up impossibly, fluffy soil with ease. Soil that exists precisely nowhere in the real world. In our dense, rocky soil? No can do.

Regardless, we were committed to MIG from day one, even though the summer droughts required us to drill holes in the ground with a portable drill in order to insert a step-in post. Every summer day, we would walk seven paces, use the drill to get a step-in post into the ground, and repeat the maneuver about forty times to complete a paddock. We would repeat the procedure day in and day out until it rained. In all of 2008, that event was more elusive than a verified sighting of the Loch Ness monster!

Therefore, to contain the sheep we were limited to using the same configuration of step-in posts and twine that kept the cows happily confined. With our portable energizers powered simply by twelve-volt marine batteries, we could generate up to 8,000 volts on the electric fence, well more than necessary to teach a cow to never touch the fence again. Funny thing about sheep though—like the feathers on chickens, turkeys and ducks, their wool or hair acts as an insulator and as a result they think little of running through the fence. And so they did.

Not content to wait for us to move the herd at the appointed time of 4:00 p.m. each day, the sheep, eyeing greener grass and seeing no reason to not run through the strands, did simply that. Naturally, this knocked down the lines, allowing the more intellectually gifted cows to reason that they too should indulge in the new forage. So it was day after day that Liz and I would see the sheep break out. We'd run out to the pasture, round them up and drive them back in again, and again, sometimes five times a day. This distraction was on top of all the other farm chores! To prevent recurrence we took the laborious step of increasing the number of fence lines we ran from the two that we used for cows to four, and later five, for the sheep.

With the knowledge of how to achieve freedom deeply ingrained, the sheep were just as comfortable breaking out through the extra strands, and so continued to do so.

Before I share how we ultimately solved this problem without incurring any expense, let me share how we attempted to solve this problem by throwing money at it. Actually the money was thrown to the owner of a dog, in the form of a border collie trained to herd sheep. A wonderful breeder lives not too far from us and we had watched her demonstrate her dog's sheep herding skills at local events. They were a marvel to watch. After our own sheep struggles, we plunked down fifteen hundred dollars for one with a great pedigree, viewing it as a labor saving device. We named the dog Zip and the owner came to our farm to work him with us a couple of times. Using loud whistle commands or verbal herding commands such as "come by," "way to me," and "drive," the dog would accomplish marvelous feats and put the sheep right where he was told. This was too good to be true!

And so it was.

Once the owner left, both Liz and I took turns working the dog and indeed he responded to the same commands he had been given by his prior owner. Unfortunately, when the ewes saw the dog just outside their paddock, they would stare him down and stomp their feet to threaten him. "Nice try ewes," I said firmly, "but this here is a sheep herding dog, and he'll be having none of that." To teach the ewes who was boss, I gave Zip the commands to encircle, drive and put the sheep where I wanted them. Using the same tactics that he had learned on the sheep at his previous farm he did indeed encircle and approach them. Unlike at his prior farm, these sheep did not obey and stomped their feet even more.

Just then Zip showed me a new trick. He stuck his head down, made his body low and long and hightailed it for the house, parking himself on the front porch.

As he sped by me I used every command I had been taught. "DOWN! STOP! SIT! STAY!"

Nothing I said deterred Zip from his appointment with the safety of our front porch. Frustrated, I went to the house and decided we'd work on it later. I told Liz, who also worked with him only to achieve the same result. Perplexed, we called the previous owner who agreed to come out and look. As she worked him, indeed he was timid now with her also. After pondering the situation she concluded that our sheep were too aggressive for him.

The bottom line? Zip was afraid of our sheep.

Great. A herding dog that can only herd trained, gentle sheep. What good was that to us? To her credit, she arranged for someone else to buy Zip from us so Zip was, hopefully, able to go somewhere to play with nice, friendly little sheep.

As for our saga of keeping the sheep with the cows, Liz and I continued going out four to five times per day to force the sheep to stay in with the cows. Today, the sheep stay in fine with the cows at all times. How did this come to be?

Simple. We had to teach the sheep to bond with the cows. Whereas the cows could be trained to respect the fence, that approach didn't work with sheep. Our forcing them back with the cows time after time resulted in a bond being formed where the sheep saw the cows as protection. Once again, there was no shortcut. It just took day in and day out perseverance to make the sheep go back in.

I suspect many traditional farmers with far more experience than we have would see our methods of farming as quite laborious. Every day we set up new paddocks for cows and sheep and move them in. We then take down the previous day's fence. Every night we move two eggmobiles to new locations so that they are parked two to three days behind the cows, matching the growth cycle of the larvae incubating in the cow patties. We check the voltage on the pigs' fences, move the pigs' paddocks frequently, drag the cows' water trough to the new paddock, drag long hoses and connect them to spigots before collecting and hand cleaning hundreds of eggs each evening. Oh, and we milk cows every day, make and age cheese, take whey to pigs, process chickens, rabbits and turkeys on farm, deliver orders to customers and, on rare occasion, sleep.

Of course we can't deliver to customers unless we have product, which means that from time to time we have to catch cows or pigs to take for processing.

Now, catching cows is an interesting endeavor in the middle of a pasture. Think about it—how would *you* go about separating and loading a single cow from a herd in the middle of a pasture, alone? Unlike most farms we have no central corral where we sort and load all animals. When we have an appointment with a USDA processor I have no way of knowing where the cows will be on the farm that day, since we rotationally graze them far and wide. Rather, I have to hook up a livestock trailer and drive to their paddock and, regardless of how muddy the pastures may be, entice the cow onto the trailer. Exactly how does one go about accomplishing that? Many farmers load a cow onto a trailer by offering sweet feed or something she likes. Our cows never see sweet feed so putting some on the trailer is no enticement and they likely won't let us get close enough to introduce it to them. The goal of loading the cow is to ensure it is as calm and stress-free as possible. Not only does this contribute to much more tender meat, it's simply consistent with our values of treating the animals with love and respect. We use no prods, no whips, no loud noises. The goal is to simply get the cow on the trailer as quickly and quietly as possible.

It probably won't come as a surprise to learn that the first cow I had to load took me six-and-a-half hours! At 4:00 p.m. on a Sunday afternoon I backed the livestock trailer up to a paddock, opened the door and began. I got into the paddock, separated the cow I wanted by pressuring her flight zone, and guided her where I wanted her to go. I got her close to the trailer door right away and several times thereafter but the trailer was a strange place for her. Besides, all of her bovine buddies were standing behind me in the paddock and she wanted to be with them. So she'd run around, past, and almost over me to get with them.

After a couple of hours of this, Liz cleverly suggested that we string up a paddock-within-a-paddock and put her in with a buddy so that she wasn't alone. We did this, and with two of them in the area the cow was much more calm. Still she didn't want to go onboard. Patiently I waited until, finally, at 10:30 p.m., I enticed her aboard and quickly shut the door. I was exhausted, but had to get up in the wee hours to take this single cow to the processor.

Over time, we improved loading. The next time took me an hour, which I thought worthy of a celebration. Now loading often takes five or ten minutes, as we set up a makeshift paddock and chute comprised of interconnecting fence panels. We march the selected cow(s) into the chute, swing the gate door and then march the cow onto the trailer.

So I suspect conventional farmers are right. Our methods are laborious. Sometimes we stare at the local soybean fields that seem to grow by themselves in the summer with or without rain and lay bare all winter, not failing to notice that we may see a farmer in the field only a handful of days throughout the year. Perhaps we should have chosen a different farming path. Still this is the only type of farming we know and I am convinced the health of our land and animals is far better for it. After three years of multi-species MIG our pastures are much more richly diverse than what we found. Now there is no crunch, as forage is essentially all vegetative. Long gone are the brambles, stemmy weed plants and bare spots.

Granted, there is still much room for improvement and we continually battle drought. The past two summers, for instance, we've received about three inches of rain between mid-June and mid-September amid a string of days with temperatures over one hundred degrees. These conditions don't support grass growth very well, but, over time, the forages will adapt to our environment, favoring grasses with deep taproots that can access whatever minerals and moisture they need to thrive.

We spray nothing on the land and spread no fertilizer that the animals don't distribute themselves. The sheep and cows generally have great body conditions, a big improvement from the first year, and we're making progress developing the pure grass-based genetics we're looking for.

It will still be many years before we can produce a consistent supply of top-quality grass-fed beef since we insist on breeding all animals on farm, but we already produce as much lamb as we aspire to. What's the rush, anyway? There is so much life on this spot of land that was so void of it just three years ago. Cows, sheep, pigs, chickens, rabbits, geese, ducks and turkeys contently graze, scratch, dig, roost and root, all the while breathing health back into the soil. More often than not, it's a beautiful sight to behold. And more often than not, we absolutely love what we do and why we do it.

We cherish each of the moments of tranquility and beauty while we can, for we will surely need to call on them to nurse us through times that are so inexplicably gut wrenching, they cause us to question every belief we hold dear.

For indeed, farming does have a very dark side.

Nothing Like a Cozy Brood House
by Liz Young

From a Nature's Harmony Farm Blog Post, Sep 10, 2009

There is nothing like a cozy brood house on a chilly, rainy day! After a couple of months of our brood house being empty I am happy to have little babies occupying it again. Our last meat chickens left the brood house in early September and since we don't raise chickens in the winter the house has been void of fuzzy babies for what seemed like forever. I forgot how much I miss visiting the brood house and seeing day-old chicks all huddled under a warm light.

For the past month we have been collecting fertile eggs from our Black Austrolorp laying hens. We moved about eighty of them from the eggmobiles so that we could ensure that the ratio of hens to roosters was correct and to ensure that all of their eggs were fertilized and purebred. Although we do have some stray chickens that have broken away from the eggmobiles and sat on clutches of eggs in the woods to hatch out some adorable little chicken mutts, we wanted to make sure the large amount that we purposefully hatched were a pure breed in order to keep the true breed going. Each week we have put a couple of hundred eggs into the incubator and the first ones have hatched perfectly and are now residing in the brood-house. We are hatching a total of one thousand new layer chicks and it feels great to feel independent from the hatcheries. By hatching our own we ensure that the offspring are strong and well adapted to our particular environment because they come from chickens that have thrived on our farm. And we also ensure that every chick hatched—both male and female—are allowed a great life of bug hunting and dirt baths.

During the hatch days we check the incubator frequently and whenever there are any chicks that have completely dried off we carry them to the brood house. There they have a stall with wood shavings on the floor, a light with four red heat bulbs warming the air to ninety-five degrees, and some fresh water and food. We give each and every chick a drink of water to make sure they know where it is and then place them under the heat lamp. They usually spend a few hours sleeping after their hard day of breaking through their shell, but before you know it they are refreshed and running around looking for food.

One of the great things about the farm is that there are many little places of solace. For me, the first few days of a new batch of chicks in the brood house is like Heaven. Today it is cold and rainy, but I am looking forward to trekking up to the brood house where I know it is warm and dry. I'll spend some time just sitting on the floor with the cute little babies watching them play and listening to their wonderful peeping which is like a lullaby. You can't beat it!

CHAPTER 7

Farming's Dark Side

By the summer of 2008 our free-range hen population had swelled to over four hundred, consisting primarily of Rhode Island Red, Australorp, and Barred Rock hens. Casually walking among them, Liz paused and looked more closely at one of the hens.

"See how this chicken is breathing?" she asked. I looked. I saw a chicken. "Don't you see it?" she asked. "She's gasping."

I saw what she was referring to but I figured the chicken was half sleeping. Sitting still, the hen would raise her head, open her mouth, take in a lot of air and then lower her head. Indeed, she was gasping for air. Naturally, Liz then closely inspected each of the other chickens, finding a few, but not many birds mirroring that behavior. We moved on and continued our farm tour but this observation weighed heavily on Liz, and she would keep an eye on it.

A few days later it was worse—much, much worse. Virtually all hens were ill. Almost all were either coughing, gasping, had swollen sinuses or had nasal discharges. It was as if the whole farm was sick. We continued walking among the hens until we saw the seven dead hens lying under the eggmobile.

We frantically searched websites for clues to see what was the likely cause and what we may be able to do about it. We identified the probable culprit as Mycoplasma infectious sinusitis, a chronic respiratory disease that spreads easily among chickens, turkeys, ducks and other poultry species. Fortunately mycoplasma is easily treated with antibiotics, which is how all poultry producers keep it and other maladies under control. Unfortunately nature doesn't use antibiotics so we eschewed their use as well. Without antibiotics the prescribed treatment is depopulation of the infected stock. If you're curious what is meant by the innocuous use of the word "depopulation," it means to kill all of the infected birds.

Stunned, we decided to turn to experts for help. Liz contacted an agency in Georgia that specialized in poultry and poultry diseases. Out they trekked to the farm dressed to the nines in their white suits and hoods as if we had a radiation leak. They took back samples from birds and called the next day with their expert recommendation.

"Burn the entire flock. That's what they said," Liz relayed to me. "They want us to burn the carcasses, sterilize the eggmobiles, wait thirty days and start over!"

I stared sternly at Liz, the messenger, before lowering my head, as I didn't know what to say. We were rookie farmers for sure and here were experts giving us advice that, well, seemed a little extreme. Perhaps even barbaric. We continued with our chores and thought it over.

The next morning the field was strewn with so many dead hens that it was easier to use the loader on our tractor to remove them. We began piling the nameless hens one by one into the bucket until I stopped suddenly while clutching a lifeless Rhode Island Red hen. I didn't have to look at it, as I knew the features of this body, now a carcass, by heart—the shape, the size and the frailty. It was Penny, who would follow me around the pasture no more. It was heartbreaking.

Why didn't any of the books tell us about this side of farming? All farming books seem to paint pictures of farm life as beautiful, peaceful and tranquil. We had read books about the horrors of factory farming, but had read nothing about the horrors of natural farming!

When we took that fateful horseback riding trip in 2006 and embarked on our farm journey, we dreamed of pastoral beauty, the tranquility of nature and living a simple, honest, meaningful life. We yearned to gaze upon content animals living the lives that they were designed to live. And we found all of that. What we didn't know was about nature's very dark side and the price it would exact on our hearts, consciences and souls.

After hashing it out until we were verbally, physically and emotionally exhausted, we held firm to our values and decided to ignore the advice of the experts and not intervene. We figured the only way our animals would ever achieve true health was through building up strong immune systems, but it was a gut-wrenching decision. To not intervene meant that, at best, we'd have to endure many more of these atrocities until the animals had built up resistance to most illnesses and parasites. At worst it may not work and we might be wrong. That would be tantamount to our letting the animals needlessly suffer.

In moments like these I am quite decisive and black-and-white. Mimicking nature means mimicking nature, not propping up animals artificially. Thus making the decision to not artificially support the animals was easy for me to make. It wasn't and still isn't for Liz, as living with the short-term consequences is excruciating. After all, and let me confess what some may see as our sins here, our decision results in individual animals having to suffer, just as some animals do in the wild. But our belief was strong: the needs of the many (the species) would outweigh the needs of the few or the one.

In a bizarre twist, this black-and-white logic of mine forced me to consider whether the same set of rules should apply to us. I mean, to me and Liz. Two years into farming had produced many animals on the farm but no children for Liz and me. We had contemplated the use of fertility clinics and perhaps even *in vitro* fertilization. Now I wasn't sure. Evidently, to use the bovine vernacular, we were "open." Would we be culled in nature? Why should medical technology be employed to enable us to reproduce if nature had created us to be incapable?

These eccentric thoughts racked my mind but I couldn't let go of them. I longed for the days when I knew nothing of these thoughts and would have simply called our health care provider and sought the fertility sorcery *du jour*. Now we couldn't and so we didn't. With the animals we'd put our trust in nature and hope for the best. We'd do the same with us and keep our fingers crossed.

And so unlike industrial chicken houses there would be no bio-security sign at the entrance of our farm. Rather than attempt to create and manage an artificial environment where our animals were protected from all viruses, we would embrace all illnesses and allow our animals to build up resistance to them. It's the way of nature and it became our path as well. Our hearts would be torn with every animal that suffered on the farm but we chose to prioritize the long-term health and viability of the herd, breed and species over the individual. Indeed only the strongest would survive and breed. By September, the hens that remained had shaken off the effects of mycoplasma and would become the foundation of our breeding hens, clearly carrying forward to their offspring some natural immunity to this common infection.

On the other hand, the heritage turkeys would become as sick as the hens had been, with only the lucky ones perishing quickly. The less fortunate turkeys would have the sides of their faces swell up so grotesquely that their eyes would literally pop out of their sockets. Like war veterans who have difficulty purging visions of brutal suffering from battles fought long ago, these gruesome sights were stowing away into our subconscious far too frequently and would emerge to haunt us from here on.

As if the devastating illness with the hens wasn't bad enough, in late October I walked out in the morning mist to find twenty full-grown turkeys strewn along a ninety-yard meandering trail in the tall grass, lifeless. None were sick and none appeared to have any visible injuries, but as I examined each more closely I found a tiny slit in the throat of each of them from which their supply of blood had drained to mate with the soil. None were eaten in any way. Just brutally murdered and left there to rot. We had purchased these fully mature turkeys for ten dollars each as poults and had fed them daily since March. Pre-sold, they were set to be processed within two weeks for Thanksgiving. At an average weight of fourteen pounds we had just suffered a loss of $100 per bird, or a total of $2,000 that we counted on receiving the next month. Instead we received nothing, disposed of the carcasses, and refunded deposits to disappointed customers who would not receive the promised turkey, leaving them to think the less of the farmers who likely ruined their Thanksgiving.

Those days of farming are really, really hard.

I speculated that the perpetrator was a raccoon but the next day I discovered it was a mink, which I saw in our pasture taking its morning stroll—its very *last* morning stroll. For his final thought the mink himself may have thought that nature, in the form of me and a shotgun, was vicious.

Unfortunately the hens and turkeys weren't the only poultry problems we had to endure in 2008. With the heritage meat chickens we witnessed an event far, far worse. And if you are squeamish I implore you to *skip this section,* for the following paragraphs graphically depict the occasional reality of natural farming.

Initially we were pleased to observe no signs of mycoplasma among the meat birds, a blessing that we attributed to the fact that these birds were younger. Indeed, we only observed it among the layers and turkeys when they reached several months of age and these meat chickens normally did not live that long. Still, we did see one chicken with a condition so unimaginable, it caused us to stop dead in our tracks. Viewed from the front or sides, this chicken appeared perfectly normal, walking around as alert as the healthiest chicken. It was simply hunting insects and eating grass. A view from the rear, however, showcased a large opening that, astonishingly, made her innards visible. It was surreal. Where we really seeing this? Was I really seeing with my eyes what my mind said I was seeing? We placed her in a cage we set up near the house, a sort of sick bay that would be overbooked for the next two years with chickens, turkeys, lambs and even pigs that had a hard time adjusting to nature's non-negotiable set of rules. This chicken, however, would not recover.

The next day all hell broke loose.

Overnight, hundreds of chickens casually but incessantly began pecking one another just above each other's anus, slowly opening golf-ball-size holes that others would peck and enlarge until, slowly over a couple of days, each bird succumbed. Indeed, a bird with an opening in the rear would peck the rear of another bird while its own rear opening was the object of curiosity for others, forming a daisy chain of carnivory! Normally this symptom of being carnivorous is the result of birds being either too crowded or having a diet too low in protein. Neither was the cause in this case as these birds enjoyed a high-protein diet, natural forage and insects, and were not in chicken tractors. Rather they were allowed to completely free-range on pasture without any netting. Yet the red broilers cannibalized one another until nary a one was left. We feverishly called hatcheries for help, posted on poultry forums and researched into the late of night. All to no avail. In the end the task of picking up buckets of dead birds each day and hauling them to the compost pile was left to Liz and me. In 2008 this became the rule rather than the exception.

In vegetable farming this would be referred to as crop failure, which has an equally devastating financial impact on the farmer. I have a hard time imagining that the emotional impact is the same. We've lost heads of broccoli. It isn't the same.

I know that many people view family farming as quaint, peaceful and pastoral, and it isn't my intention to shatter that vision. Indeed it is all that but the fact is that natural, sustainable farming, with all of the beautiful moments that we all long for, is not immune to the cycle of life and death. In nature, death can seem cruel when viewed through a human's perspective but most of the time it is hidden from us. We see the raccoons, deer, rabbits, squirrels and opossums in the fields, climbing the trees and crossing the roads. We don't see the ones in the woods that die violently or couldn't make it on their own, therefore being left to suffer, alone. Now we were immersed in nature and witness to all of her fury. And glory. We were granted no access to one without the other; a fact that has somewhat hardened our perspective as farmers. Nature endows us with today's sun on the beach as she brews tomorrow's hurricane. If we wish to bask in one we must endure the other.

Of course one could attempt to circumvent the dark side of farming by creating artificial environments, controlling light and temperature, and feeding vitamins, antibiotics and vaccines, propping up a non-sustainable Potemkin village of animal husbandry. Such a slippery slope descends into the abyss of factory farming, which is as far away from a natural existence as one could imagine an animal living. A cold, hard reality weighed heavily on us as we finally embraced, with heads hung low, that we couldn't have it both ways if we farmed in harmony with nature.

Harmony. What does the word really mean? It has a rather pleasing sound to it and the word "pleasing" is often used to describe the meaning of the word. But what pleases nature?

Balance pleases nature.

If balance is achieved by letting the strong survive and letting the weak morph into organic matter then it is decreed without conscious, without regret and without intervention. Nature's model encourages sows to give birth in the wild to more piglets than will actually survive, thus stacking the odds in favor of perpetuating the species. Why? Because it is expected that some will be too weak to survive or that some will be needed to feed the diversity of nature's predators and scavengers, and this is the price that nature exacts for allowing the bountiful production of piglets. Ditto with turtles, chicks, penguins, lion cubs and every species on earth.

Why then should we not expect and embrace the same results in any environment that supports life? Why are we so shocked and alarmed to find a farm animal that withers, suffers and succumbs? I suspect that we may have suffered more on our farm in this regard than on most farms since we opt to not offer any "unnatural" support in the form of vaccines, antibiotics, dewormers and the like, thereby effectively bringing any suffering on ourselves. We completely understand why other farmers intervene and help. As animal lovers, more often than not we wish we did. It would sure be easier on us. For what we're trying to accomplish however, that would be a band-aid solution that would require perpetual application. As hard as this medicine was to swallow we chose to swallow hard and hope for a long-term cure, only now we were dealing with the bitter taste of the medicine.

In this age of increased support of local food and sustainable farming, it's common for the public to respect farmers who farm in accordance with nature's principles. Indeed, consumers seem to admire them and elevate some to a type of rock-star status. But these farms are often half-viewed through pastoral lenses that conveniently allow consumers to take in images of contented animals, while rendering images of the darker side of farming as visible only to the farmer. For that reason I opted to not choose for the cover of this book a picture of me carrying a dead chicken to the compost pile. Yet it is as real a part of farming as any tranquil walk through the pasture.

Nature offers no explanation and takes no mercy in its culling decisions any more than gardeners do when they thin (cull) their rows of carrot seedlings. But because we deal with animal life we are required to explain our decisions, lest we be judged even more harshly. So while I may feel the need to apologize for exposing this dark side to you the fact is that farmers have to live with this reality every day, and this is where food comes from. And I'm sad to say that there's more depressing news to come.

Four times I've had to contort myself in the slippery muck, using strength I knew not that I had, to pull, push and roll a full-grown, thousand-pound dead cow into the bucket of my tractor, so I could dispose of her. Four times in the past year. By myself. Each time the event occurred after futile efforts on our part to save the cow.

For reasons we don't usually understand, cows sometimes lie down and can't or won't get up. They lie there, happily grazing and appearing fine but can't get to their feet. It's important that we get them up immediately. To do so, we push, prod and poke the cow in an effort to save her life. If those measures don't work, we lower the tractor bucket until it's a foot or so above her, wrap hip hooks or straps around her hip bones and use the tractor to lift her up. This is the approach prescribed to us by experienced farmers and veterinarians, many of whom are old-timers who also tell us, "That's a Jersey for you—they just lay down and die!" Regardless, in our experience, the measures we attempt have never worked, for the cow went down for a reason. But what was the reason?

Often the cause of the cow going down, particularly in dairy operations, is suspected to be hypocalcemia, more commonly referred to as milk fever. Milk fever is a condition of calcium deficiency and generally occurs around the time of calving. Indeed, one of the cows we lost was a dairy cow and it was right at the time of calving. The other cows we lost were also dairy cows, but none were near calving time. When milk fever is suspected, the recommendation is to administer calcium gluconate, which is simply calcium and glucose.

But there are other potential causes besides milk fever. It could be grass tetany which has very similar clinical signs to milk fever. Tetany, often a fatal metabolic disorder, results from low levels of magnesium in the bovine's blood. More often than not, it occurs during grazing of succulent, springtime forages and affects even the best cows in the herd.[9]

However, none of our cows went down during times of fresh, succulent forage.

Then again it could be nitrate poisoning, which can occur when cows eat forages with high levels of nitrates, such as brassicas or clover. When large amounts of nitrates are eaten in a very short period of time, nitrates are absorbed into the blood after being accumulated in the rumen. If the nitrates do in fact enter the bloodstream, they can bind with red blood cells, interfering with their ability to bind oxygen.[10]

Or it could be...who knows. An edict of our farming model and values is that we, like nature, do not use veterinarians. Yet our human need to know what's happening in our environment has prompted us on a few occasions to call vets to the farm. Not for the purpose of treating. For the purpose of diagnosing and explaining just so we can understand. Four times they've come. Four times they've not been able to tell us what the problem was. It "may be" milk fever, or it "may be" tetany, or it "may be" something else.

All of this just stunned us as new farmers. You mean to tell us that you can't just put cows out on pasture, let them graze the way nature intended and all will be well with the universe? No, these "new" cows are so far removed from those that may have been raised naturally a century ago, we were clearly starting from scratch.

We always feel so helpless in these situations. We can't get the cow to stand up and are forced to comfort her even though we're told that if she's down for a day or more, she won't get up. Ever. Indeed, that's our experience as well. The vets seem to not know what to do other than recommend hit or miss broad-spectrum antibiotics. So we feel alone and tie ourselves into knots trying to decide what is right.

Would it be most humane to shoot the cow, which we are often advised to do?

Indeed I have had to do this twice, each time by drawing an imaginary line from each eye to the opposite ear, and placing a bullet where the lines intersect. Nothing in my business career prepared me for this and the image of the cow I just shot imprints firmly in my sub-conscious. Later as I'm smiling and talking to a customer at a farmers market, it can abruptly reveal itself to me uninvited. My smile vanishes as I gaze off in the distance, seeing not the customer, but a wildly thrashing cow with blood gushing from its nostrils, leaving the customer to drift away wondering what they said.

Would it be right to not shoot the cow, to give her an opportunity to be "that" miracle who rose to her feet after being down for a week? I've tried that too as we brought water and hay to a cow who was down for ten days. Each day, other than the fact that she was down, the cow seemed alert and content. But she never rose and as the end neared began convulsing and thrashing. So it was as my heavy heart summoned the pistol, my finger pulled the trigger and my numb shell of a body was the accomplice. Dazed, I pushed her into my tractor bucket and had no idea why.

Then again we've had pigs that had severe cases of parasite overload and instead of pulling the trigger, granted them the opportunity to become their own miracle. And they did! But was that more humane?

In the winter of 2009-2010 we watched a pig wither to nothing, lose virtually all of his hair and walk through the woods like a skeleton for months on end. We waited and waited for him to die only to see him later recover, gain weight and achieve health. Was it humane to let the pig wither like that even though he ultimately pulled through months later? Or would it have been more humane to end his suffering even if it meant denying the creature, my brother in nature, future sentience?

The problem is that as farmers we have the means to play God in matters affecting animals and thus are required, unlike nature, to act on a conscious choice. If we do nothing, that's a choice. In the end it's easier to make the choice to not play God and just let nature decide how the game will unfold, a game in which we become imprisoned as horrified spectators bound to ringside seats.

Fortunately the memories of the downed cows can be momentarily eclipsed on the days when a cow gives birth to a calf. Even if we have to pull the calf, which is one of those things that new farmers fear, it's still a great day. As new farmers we fretted about pulling calves early on. The first time we pulled a calf, Liz, without a moment's hesitation, joined me in the pasture, inserted her gloved arm into the cow all the way up to her shoulder, grabbed the calf's hooves, and began pulling. That girl can farm!

Given all that we've now experienced the memories of having to pull calves occupy positive cells in my memory bank rather than negative ones. I'd prefer not do have to do it since nature doesn't but there are far more regrettable sides to the animal husbandry.

Like when a cow rejects her calf or a ewe rejects her lamb. Like when a calf has maggots in its anus that can't be successfully removed. Like when a calf has maggots in its infected belly near the umbilical cord that can't be extracted. Like when a ewe has a vaginal or anal prolapse.

When rejected by the mother we take the calf or lamb and bottle-feed it, a clear example of hypocrisy in our goal to truly mimic nature. Nature would let the calf die. We attempt to give it a chance by giving it milk. We draw the line at not using chemicals or medicines but we also have to try and help the infant with milk. We have to.

Still it's hypocritical if we really attempt to mimic nature 100% and we know it. Then again so is having an electric fence, and so we remember that our aim is to mimic nature within the context of healing the land and producing food with, ultimately, zero off-farm inputs. Saving this calf with milk from the farm could help with each of those objectives.

It matters not, for in this case the calf, Pollyanna, dies anyway. A beautiful, silver gray Murray Grey calf who has, for weeks now, come running energetically when we enter the paddock salivating over the bottle we held out for her, dies, inexplicably. After being completely rejected and kicked away from birth by her mother, she just dies, and so on a frosty October morning we pick up her damp, limp body, eyes open but dead and staring us in the face as a reminder that we somehow failed her. We don't want to pick her up; it's too emotionally draining. But somebody has to and we are always that somebody.

The same month, October 2009, we sigh in relief when the forecast is that we will once again get some rain. The summer just ended was harsh, once again, leaving pastures parched. Evidently nature believed she owed us some rain, and she delivered. Just weeks prior some areas near Atlanta had received up to twenty inches of rain in one day, something the media enjoyed labeling as a 500-year flood. Like anyone could even know that. People lost their lives, bottomland farmers lost their topsoil and everyone was trying to recover. Now, nature delivered a flood to us, several inches of rain within a few hours. Due to the composition of our soil, an inch of rain is about like three inches of rain and that is not hyperbole. This fact makes it possible for us to survive the summer. Since drainage is so poor the soil does hold moisture, allowing grasses to hang on in the oppressive heat. Still, on this day we received over five inches of rain, which produced raging flash floods even though our land is reasonably high and sloping.

We weren't worried about losing topsoil. We were worried about losing lives.

Liz and I donned our best rain gear and walked the farm, taking the wind-driven rain to the face like tiny daggers. We couldn't cross the creek to get off the farm as little Sally's creek had turned into a river, rising over ten feet and easily cresting her banks, destroying our orchard and discarding our permanent woven-wire fence and cemented-wooden posts like they were simply tooth picks. We called our apprentices, Kerry and Amanda, and asked them to check on the animals at the front of the farm since their housing was on the other side of the creek.

Liz and I walked through the hardwoods high up on the hill where the sow paddock was. One of our last Berkshire sows, Daisy, the only female survivor from Dottie's first litter, had just delivered a litter of ten piglets the day before. As we entered the woods our eyes grew wide, becoming filled with the nightmare of an impromptu, raging creek where no stream had been before. Daisy and the sows were on the opposite side.

We stepped into the creek, hugging slippery trees for balance, and quickly plunged waist deep in an astonishingly fast flowing current. Out of nowhere visions of those cliffhanger rescue shows on TV flashed through my mind. Climbing out we sought other paths in an effort to help the sows and piglets stranded on something of an island in the middle of the woods. The woods were dark and filled with moving water so we couldn't tell if the water was shallow on the surface or if there were deep pockets filled with water. The woods that looked so familiar the day before became unrecognizable and filled us with panic that day. The rescue attempt would not be without danger.

Placing slippery logs over the makeshift creek we managed to crawl across. We tried to corral the sows and piglets and drive them to cross but these attempts proved futile. We searched for Daisy and found her in the rear of the paddock. She had built her nest in the worst place of all, a low spot—a low spot where ten drowned Berkshire piglets now lay dead. Daisy was our last hope in an effort to breed maternal instincts into our Berkshires and indeed she had taken to her piglets when they were born. But when nature intervened the Berkshire sow did nothing to protect her young as the Ossabaw sows did with their young, none of which perished in the flood. How could a mother pig have no instincts to walk her babies up a slope when a flood came?

Dammit! We've become so sick of this! I wanted to just block it out but the vision beat me in the race by imprinting itself quickly and filing the memory away atop the others: dead piglets strewn among the leaves, once again.

Why do we farm this way if it's so physically and emotionally stressful on the animals and us? Why not just provide housing, dewormers and antibiotics to our livestock, just like we would do for a family member who needed it? It's a fair question.

Is it normal for most other farms to endure the misfortunes I've described? No, I don't think so. If, as a society, we were able to gaze upon two farming models side by side with one being your typical CAFO and the other being all animals in their natural habitat, I believe an overwhelming majority would have a strong emotional repulsion from the former and a strong emotional bond with the latter. After all, it is beautiful to see rare turkeys and pigs (not the industrial breeds) ranging on pasture and in the woods with the pastures providing a natural habitat for cows, sheep, chickens, rabbits and the like.

This is the model to which we are all emotionally drawn, but the problem is that we, as a society, have allowed most of our animals to be farmed industrially over the better part of the last century. Even the animals that have been farmed in smaller family farm settings have been supported as needed with vaccines, antibiotics and care. This may have been done in the name of love and compassion, but was dosed out with an unintended consequence; many animals became so dependent on us that they can't survive, even in their natural habitat, without human assistance. For we had all modified their habitat so greatly that it now required food to be brought to them, medicines to be forced upon them, and climates controlled for them. Again, this is true on even small family farms, as evidenced by giving blankets to horses or bringing animals into a barn in winter. Whether it's a chicken, pig, turkey or cow, we have all, by virtue of encouraging cheap food at any cost, participated in reshaping the genetic makeup of all farm animals to the point where virtually no species can thrive in a natural setting. Even though we collectively want to see farm animals raised in natural settings the fact is, as we have learned dearly, that the ability to do so must be re-learned. This is the case even with rare-breed heritage animals, although they have a substantial advantage over industrial breeds.

Just as with a decision to stop smoking, we decided to put our animals back to their habitat cold turkey, if you will. We make sure their environment has access to food, access to shelter and access to water. That's it. We don't make them eat the food, seek the shelter or drink the water. If they don't have the survival skills to seek shelter from a blazing sun or a fierce storm, nature can decide if they survive, breed and perpetuate those traits.

So despite the emotional toll we believe it is not only right to return animals to their natural setting without any support, but that it is also the only way a farm can become truly eco-logically sustainable. Still, it's insane to us that we have had to suffer so much loss in pursuit of such a simple goal as return-ing animals to a natural setting. Regardless of the ongoing emotional and financial toll, we feel that we can't give in on our dogged pursuit of this goal, yet there are so many times when we want to. We moved out here out of love for animals, the same love that caused us to take up farming. We've picked up so many dead chickens, so many dead, limp piglets, so many dead cows and calves. So much *death*—it erodes us, it hardens us, it allows doubt to creep in and this often confuses us.

Yet we march on, inspired by some signs that the path we're walking, albeit strewn with so much mortality, is the right path. Three years after our initial outbreak of mycoplasma our closed flock of chickens and turkeys, all of which were bred and hatched on our farm, are remarkably healthy and vigorous. Feathers and eyes are bright and rarely do we see any effects of the respiratory illness that prompted the recommendation to depopulate our flocks. We were right to ignore that and to breed the survivors, with our birds now having built up resistance to blackhead, mycoplasma and other ailments just as they would in natural settings.

Still, even though our adult cows have adjusted well to the forage-only diet of our land, as evidenced by their sleek coats and excellent body condition, we still suffer calf losses. Some baby calves may live for six or eight months or more, looking weak and wormy the entire time, only to finally succumb. Indeed the gestation cycle is much longer on a cow (over nine months) than a pig (over three months), and certainly much longer than a chicken (less than one month), so it's sensible that it will take much longer for us to achieve the natural acclimations we seek among the cows. Understanding this I now harden myself knowing full well that nature will bestow upon us an abundant gift of beautiful Murray Grey and Jersey calves next year, and then rescind the offer on a precious few only after we've accepted and bonded with the gift.

The point is this: the emotional cost to produce meat from animals that are truly raised naturally is a very high one for the farmer. The choices we must make are difficult, the alternatives unclear. Such is the responsibility of the natural farmer. I didn't fully appreciate this fact back on the golf course as I ordered a burger from the grill and probably grumbled about the price. I do fully appreciate it now.

The cost to reconnect animals to live in natural settings without human support is a debt that many animals in transition must honor with their lives. Many consumers may not have an appreciation for these emotional costs, as they remain blissfully unaware, as we used to be, while seeing a farmer at the farmers' market or taking in the pristine beauty of the landscape when they visit the farm. Still, the debt to nature must be honored and will be repaid over a period of many years by the farmer, for the debt was incurred over decades by producing industrial breed animals that lost all ability to live in nature. This was mankind's fault and we felt it became our responsibility to remedy.

If you're a farmer you know about such things, of course. Cows will go down. Piglets will be stepped on. Hawks will bite the heads off chickens and leave the remaining carcass untouched. Ewes will reject lambs. The question is, how are farmers to respond to this reality? Some, quite understandably, intervene. When they do, will they ever be able to break the habit of doing so? Will the breeds and species become increasingly dependent on them and lose their ability to live, let alone thrive, on their own?

We each have to answer those questions for ourselves.

It's so easy to give up. It's so easy to intervene and prop the animals up with antibiotics. Is it really so wrong to do either? The more we farmed, the harder the questions became. The question we kept asking ourselves after our first two years of farming was this: why on earth were we so hell-bent on doing everything the hard way?

LONGING FOR CONNECTION
BY TIM YOUNG

From a Nature's Harmony Farm Blog Post, May 5, 2010

What is it that so many of us are missing in our lives? I'm continually intrigued by the amount of interest there is in farming, getting back to the land and getting reconnected with our food. "Re"connected actually is inaccurate, since most of us have never been connected in the first place, but it refers to us more as a species rather than individuals. What exactly are we all trying to get connected to? The land? Our own food? Community? Each other? Are we just trying to make sense of it all?

This back-to-the-land movement, of course, began over twenty years ago with a few brave souls. If any of you corporate types are familiar with Geoffrey Moore's marketing classic *Crossing the Chasm*, you'll recognize this group as innovators and early adopters. Moore's "chasm theory" described for readers why hi-tech products initially sold well, but then suffered. It's because in any movement there are innovators and early adopters, basically evangelists who don't really need to be sold but rather want the next great thing, followed by early majority, late majority, and laggards, all on the other side of the chasm, who require a different sales and messaging approach. Have we crossed the chasm now, or is this a new phase in which people like us and others are today's innovators and early adopters?

Farming...the word itself can often conjure up images of hard work, little money and little time for yourself. A slight twist on the word, changing it to homesteading, conjures up feelings of freedom, independence and control. During tours and customer visits, I often describe Nature's Harmony Farm as less of a farm and more of a large homestead that homesteads for a large group of people. Semantics, I suppose, but it's why we're into so many things (bees, cheese, cured meats, milk, eggs, veggies, fruit, vineyard, all species of animals, etc.), because that makes good homesteading sense, and not necessarily good economic farming sense.

I digress, I suppose.

I'm pondering that this morning as I look at all the registrants we have so far for our Farm School in July and see all the comments on our Farmcast on iTunes, where there are almost fifty written reviews. Our farm tour this month is once again booked with about sixty people, and our butchering, cheese-making and curing classes all filled up quickly. It's clear that there is a lot of interest in many of the things we are experiencing. Not just farming, but food preservation, learning lost skills, finding independence and living more connected with nature.

Or am I wrong? Is it something else? Something deeper and more elusive. What is it that so many feel is lacking or missing in their lives that creates interest in this lifestyle?

I'm not sure, but I look forward to reading your comments. They say the grass is always greener. I'm pretty happy with the grass on our side of the fence.

CHAPTER 8

Value-Based Farming

From a farmer's point of view, nature can be very, very cruel, and maddeningly inexplicable in her actions. She sentences us to long periods of drought so severe a drill bit can't be powered into the ground. The air becomes so dry, dusty and void of breath, that pervasive lethargy envelops the farm and all hope seems lost. Then she grows bored with drought and delivers to us torrential rains that form a raging flood, thinking it will quench our thirst.

We pray for drought again.

On the rare days that everything seems perfect, with the grass soft and green, the skies clear and blue and the animals happy and healthy, we notice, and are deeply appreciative. As a farmer it seems as if we cast two shadows, one of despair and the other of hope. The best days in a farmer's life are hard, but rewarding, and each day begins with hope anew.

The fact that nature can be cruel is something we all understand abstractly, but Liz and I have found out many times over how cruel she can be and how strong the temptation is to intervene and change nature's will. Never is this temptation greater than when an animal's life is at stake.

This book details beautiful stories of birth, life and happiness. Yet the previous chapter revealed the darker side of farming, recounting horrid stories of suffering, death and despair. Could there be a more accurate description of nature's blessings and fury than those two sentences? How does one get through the times of such utter discouragement that leaves them filled with doubt, questions, anger and grief?

The answer is faith, and our faith is in our values.

From the outset, our desire was to mimic nature within an agricultural context, although we knew we'd have a perimeter fence around our world. While there are no fences in nature other than seashores, we set out to respect and emulate nature to the fullest extent possible on our farm. I'll admit that this goal is somewhat idealistic, but we at least wanted to start with the intention of orchestrating an environment where animals were truly raised as they were intended in harmony with nature. It was that goal that inspired Liz to come up with the name for our new farm, Nature's Harmony Farm.

Before we started with animals, we had read about other farmers who used the phrase "mimicking nature" and so we observed their farming practices. In many ways, the farming model was inventive and represented a definite improvement over factory farming. Cows, chickens, pigs, turkeys, rabbits and more were being raised in relatively natural conditions. That is to say, on pasture or in woods. There was no fertility problem on these farms as animals grazed forage offered by the land or local feed that was imported, and returned organic matter directly where it belonged, on the land.

If they were of the laying variety, chickens were free to roam, scratch, hunt, roost and take dust baths. Pigs had freedom to root and wallow, activities which rank high on any pig's list of most treasured pastimes. While the pigs seemed to enjoy life, upon closer examination, the male pigs weren't exactly having a ball. Literally. They had each been castrated at a very young age, traumatically, I suspect, and without anesthesia. The farmer we visited could claim plausible deniability in this case as none of the pigs were born on his farm, having bought weaned piglets from another farmer who dealt with the dirty work of castration. No doubt that approach is easier than managing breeders but it wasn't my idea of natural farming.

As we looked deeper, both at the farming model we were examining and into our hearts for guidance, other concerns emerged that, for us at least, were incongruent with mimicking nature. I mentioned that the laying hen could roost, scratch, hunt and range. Her counterpart, the broiler, or meat chicken, wasn't quite as fortunate. While it's true that the broiler was on pasture, it was closely confined, as is the case on many pastured poultry farms. Its incarceration took the form of a mobile chicken tractor that was less than two feet in height. This gave the broiler about a foot of headroom, and, maybe, one and a half square feet per bird of fresh pasture each day.

That doesn't sound so bad, and indeed does represent somewhat of an improvement over overcrowded chicken houses, but wasn't the chicken still being held closely confined? Could the chicken really express its chicken-ness in a space where it couldn't even roost, something all chickens are of want to do? I suspect that through the eyes of a chicken, close confinement on pasture is, at best, a very slight improvement over close confinement indoors. After all, close confinement is close confinement, whether it's on pasture or in a shed.

Then again the farm we visited, like many pastured poultry producers, raised the same white industrial breed chickens that can be found in overcrowded factory farms. Having been bred for climate control I am not convinced that these birds are actually happier being outside. In fact, I don't believe they are. Indeed, we experimented with them our first year just to make sure we weren't being hypocritical by not giving the breed a chance. We weren't, for anytime we received a strong rainstorm, dozens and dozens of Cornish X (pronounced Cornish Cross) would lie dead in the pastures among the heritage breeds we also raised, which suffered no casualties. The frailty we observed with industrial breeds was far from a singular experience, and in the end we concluded it wasn't humane to raise industrial breeds in our model.

We also had read that broilers in chicken tractors consume many insects as part of their diet. We examined the model and observed that grasshoppers and crickets were pretty adept at not jumping into the chicken tractors, instead playing safely out of range where the broiler, sentenced to confinement, watched mildly bewildered. The one and a half square feet of fresh pasture the broiler was allotted each morning in the chicken tractor quickly became soiled as the voracious eaters put away some grass and a tremendous quantity of chicken feed. It has to go somewhere. It does, and they lie in it. While the soil was being enriched we thought that perhaps that could be accomplished without the chickens having to lie in their excrement. If the goal is to let a chicken be a chicken, we asked ourselves, does the chicken prefer to be confined that closely or to free-range within a much larger area? We pondered the question but our values began to solidify firmly in favor of the animals and nature.

Beyond the choice of breeds there was another intriguing part of operating a farm that we became curious about. Farmers sometimes embrace a policy of refusing to ship product anywhere since it could be offered by local farmers in distant markets, negating any need for shipping and thereby not harming the environment. This is great environmental leadership by these farmers, in my view, as biologically sustainable farming is indeed a local business. At the same time the same farmers buy day-old chicks from distant hatcheries and have those chicks shipped through the mail every week. Why? The farmers are more than capable of maintaining their own breeding flock as farmers did in the past and hatching out on farm. If a farmer is truly interested in sustainability and mimicking nature, why would they ship in poultry instead of hatching them on farm, but refuse to ship product out? That seemed really hypocritical to me.

There's another dirty little secret to consider about hatcheries that isn't discussed frequently. When a farmer or homesteader wants to increase their laying flock and orders chicks from a hatchery, it comes as no surprise that female chicks are desired instead of male. Hatcheries are highly skilled at sexing, or determining the sex right when chicks are born, and thus pack the female chicks for shipment. What happens to the male chicks of the laying breed variety? They are killed upon hatching, often by being ground alive. Their life includes being hatched, handled by a human to determine their bad luck at being male, and then tossed into an auger where they are chopped up. If you have the stomach for this, there's a video at www.naturesharmonyfarm.com that shows the process. Just search on "male chicks ground alive."

Of course most people are unaware of this but now you are. Whether we all turn our heads or stare the truth in the face, the fact is that if we buy laying hens from hatcheries, we condone or, at the very least, acquiesce with this practice. Similarly, when we pat ourselves on the back for buying eggs at farmers markets from farmers who buy their hens from hatcheries we're still complicit in the act. The beauty of living in a free society is that we all get to decide our own values, and I decided that the little rooster deserved a shot at life. Nature decrees that some of the offspring will be male and a percentage will be female, so what right do we have to exterminate them upon arrival simply because they're not what we wished for? Damn our collective sense of entitlement and pursuit of control! Surely, with all of our human ingenuity, we can find a way to give the little roosters a good life, and figure out how to make them good on the table. For our part we are attempting to and indeed half of the "hens" roaming the pastures at Nature's Harmony Farm are roosters.

As we digested all these issues we cemented another value. We would endeavor to create a farm that gave birth to every animal, allowed it to live naturally, and, when harvested, ensured it died as quickly and humanely as possible. Sure we had to buy some breeder stock to begin with but from then on we aimed to orchestrate a farm where life began, flourished and ended. Making this decision essentially forced our hand on the next key value decision we made, which related to the breeds we selected.

Commercial chicken houses, as stated previously, rely primarily on the Cornish X chicken, or closely related strains of Ross or Cobb chickens. Make no mistake; these remarkable birds have been genetically selected and designed to grow at alarming rates. Their feed conversion is better than two-to-one, resulting in one pound of weight gain for every two pounds of feed consumed. Larger pastured poultry producers overwhelmingly support the use of the industrial Cornish X chicken and indeed these white behemoths are the variety most found in chicken tractors. If it strikes you as odd that industrial confinement breeds are being raised in a "natural" setting, it did us as well.

These birds were bred for climate control and a quick web search on "Cornish X problems" or "Cornish X horror" will enlighten you as to the problems most experience with this breed. This problem can be masked in the short-term by lacing feed with extra vitamins, antibiotics and supplements, but then again, that doesn't fit with my definition of biological sustainability.

It's ironic indeed to champion a natural, pastoral, nature-mimicking model and yet to deploy fast growing, industrial breeds that are shipped in from distant hatcheries. In this model, the factory-farmed chicken lives thirty-nine days compared to forty-two days in the larger pastured poultry farms. Three extra days of cramped confinement. Yippee.

For me, raising an industrial hybrid breed chicken in a chicken tractor could be viewed as factory farming on pasture. Nothing is "natural" about a Cornish X chicken. Of course, this doesn't mean that all farmers *want* to raise the Cornish X, but even those who don't likely feel as if they are forced into a trap. Some see the same problems with the breed that I've mentioned yet feel as if they have no alternative. A farmer can't buy Cornish X breeders and can't breed the chicks they buy since the Cornish X is a hybrid of different breeds. If they bred the baby chicks, they would get very inconsistent results in growth, efficiency and vigor. The only choice therefore is for a farmer is to buy day-old Cornish X chicks from a hatchery and grow them out, or to buy slow-growing breeds that have a far worse feed conversion ratio, resulting in a higher price and reduced cash flow.

Consumers, thanks to the efficacy of industrial food marketers over recent decades, have become accustomed to chickens that not only have big, meaty breasts, but are cheap, bloodless, boneless, and cut up to boot. Conveniently, these marketers are generally under the employ of the corporation that owns the breeder chickens, and the consumer ends up with virtually no choice. Sure they can choose Tyson or Perdue, but both use similar fast-growing genetic Frankenstein breeds.

Since consumers have come to expect this, a small farmer is faced with either giving them the fast growing industrial bird that they expect, albeit raised on pasture, or undertaking a laborious commitment to the education required to inform and persuade consumers to purchase a more expensive, slower-growing, less uniform breed. Farming is hard enough and very few farmers have the appetite to confront such a challenge.

We decided early on to take on that assignment because we knew that in order to mimic nature and achieve real sustainability, we would need breeds that could thrive in our environment. Factory-farmed breeds are about as natural on pasture as ammonia nitrate, with both providing a momentary and unsustainable illusion of success.

As we suffered through all of the issues with animal mortality, slow growth rates, difficulty in developing breeders of multiple species, and repeated early failures with breeding in maternal instincts, we just wanted to throw up our hands and quit so many times. So why didn't we just give up or give in? Why don't we now?

Sustainability is a word that is thrown around a lot regarding farming and indeed its popularity has caught the attention, once again, of industrial food marketers. We had to wrestle with what the word "sustainability" meant to us and ultimately defined two primary limbs of sustainability: economic and biological.

Economic sustainability should be self-evident and requires a partnership with supporting consumers. If the farm can't operate profitably, no matter how high its ideals, it will fail, dealing a blow to both the farmer and the community food shed. So from the get-go we valued economic sustainability, but always made that a secondary consideration to what we felt was more important and elusive, and that was biological sustainability.

To my way of thinking biological sustainability means that the farm can endure indefinitely because it does not depend on off-farm inputs and the effect of its operation is that it creates more food, diversity and fertility each passing year. Why diversity? Because diversity reduces risk and nature is rich with diversity. Because we are omnivores and evolved by consuming a diverse diet, including meat. In turn, the farm should put forth a diverse forage smorgasbord for its diners that should constitute a diverse representation of nature's creations.

The biologically sustainable farm can endure and enrich at the same time because it is a holistic model that creates no waste while enriching the land. In turn this produces better grass, forage or plants, which further nourish the eater each year better than the prior year.

Since the eaters on our farm would be animals and our definition of long-term biological sustainability decreed no off-farm inputs, a commitment to developing our own breeds or preserving heritage breeds was required. We had to say "no" to breeds such as Cornish X because there was no way to breed them ourselves. If we wanted a chicken dinner we would have to, as farmers had done decades ago, develop our own breeds of meat chickens, hatch them on farm and build up hardiness.

Heritage and older breeds have preserved many more of the traits necessary to survive in a natural setting than the modern breeds, which are engineered to survive, not thrive, in a factory farm setting. Maternal instincts are not an asset for a factory-farmed pig, and indeed are a liability as the owner doesn't want a screaming sow wanting to get with her young, so that trait is bred out. The good news is that the older breeds are not only far hardier, they are far more delicious than anything to be found at the supermarket.

Similarly, feedlot cattle have been bred up in size over decades for one simple reason. You can hang more meat on their frame, which is easy to do when you're feeding them thirty-two pounds of a grain-antibiotic mix every day. Take the same large frame cows and put them on grass-only and they physically can't ingest enough grass each day to gain the weight necessary to finish.

The choices we were forced to carefully consider became more complex and more clear at the same time. We knew that to give the animals a great life we had to choose breeds that were able to live without being propped up by humans. It sounds nice to put pigs in the woods and let them have their own young, but if the mother has no maternal instincts and abandons her young, then is this not both pointless and cruel to the young? Some of the breeds and the individual animals we originally selected had turned out to not be good mothers. They had received little help from us, just as no one helps wild pigs with their young. Now we were facing the emotional and financial consequences of this reality.

For sure, all the piglets we lost meant lots of money lost but the larger and more enduring cost was the emotional toll it took on us. Time after time in our first two years, we picked up cold, dead piglets no bigger than our hands. I wasn't sure how much more we could take.

"Why don't we just homestead? Why do we have to have all these animals and farm for everybody else?" Liz was clearly emotionally raw by the death of a trio of Berkshire piglets. We lost the death count on piglets long, long ago.

I answered her question quickly, but I should have given it more thought. It's a good question.

Why *are* we doing this? When we set out to move to the country we never set out to farm anyway. We certainly never set out to feed the world. We felt a calling to live in the country and we wanted the tranquil and simple life it promised. Liz has always just wanted to homestead and, she says, be a hermit. I am not completely sure that I want to be hermit but I am completely sure that carrying dead chickens and piglets to the compost pile is not tranquil.

"We're doing this for the animals, sweetie," I offer softly and calmly. "We're doing this for the land. We're doing this for all the customers who care about the animals and who want clean, nutritious food, but can't farm themselves. We're doing this because if people like us don't then we're all approving of factory farms."

She looks at me suspiciously and I know what she's thinking. She's thinking that if we're doing this for the animals then why are some dying. I try to explain, once again, that while it's painful for me to watch an animal not make it, my efforts are focused on the health of the herd and the breed, not the individual. I believe in our path, and indeed I've seen the results with our poultry. But it takes much longer to get there with longer gestation animals such as cows, sheep and pigs. I walk to the other room, sigh where Liz can't hear me and prepare to have the discussion once again the next time an animal is in peril. I pray it won't be anytime too soon.

I believe all of this and I know full well how very fortunate we are to have a piece of land. I'm so grateful for that gift and as a result, we should do our best to improve it ecologically, use it to produce an abundant supply of clean, healthy food and let it be a playground for all the animals we love so much.

It would be easier to not farm, for sure. Liz is right but so am I. We carry on, fueled by all the wonderful, blissful moments we have on the farm, for while there may have been some animals that did not fare well, our farm is full of animals bouncing happily and healthily through woods and across pastures. Despite the fact that she doesn't always see it, these numbers far exceed the number of animals that struggle.

Prior to farming, we read about industrial food production and the massive amounts of antibiotics that were administered and fed to animals, and became alarmed. It seemed clear to us that this futile attempt to control nature would result in a backlash of antibiotic resistant viruses and bacteria. Did we learn nothing from Darwin?

To us caring for and protecting the animals meant developing herds that were remarkably healthy and that had strong immune systems. We concluded that we could best achieve this by not "propping them up" with medical and excessive human support, so we made a very firm commitment to not provide vaccines, antibiotics or chemical dewormers under any circumstances. We chose to trust nature and put our faith in her. We would orchestrate a natural environment for the animals, but in the end, natural selection would decide which individuals thrived and which didn't.

The deaths we had experienced on the farm had hardened us. Rather than throwing in the towel or taking the easy way out, our resolve somehow strengthened. It was so outrageous that animals couldn't live naturally that we became even more determined to help the animals get to the point where they could. And, after three years of farming this way, I think this approach is working. On this farm there have been many joyous moments of birth, bonding, and celebrations of life. It is true that moments of death harden us but they are outweighed on the mortality seesaw by adorable little piglets nursing their mother in green summer pastures, by bouncing baby lambs stopping playtime only long enough to get a drink from the mother ship, by heritage turkeys walking in tall grass with poults they hatched out on their own, and by charming baby rabbits snuggled deep in a nest of fur that their mother tugged from her chest. These moments warm our hearts, change our perspective and keep us in unrelenting pursuit of developing the strong hardy breeds needed to achieve biological sustainability.

We will continue this pursuit of reconnecting our animals with their natural environments, allowing the best to breed and continually evolve strong maternal instincts, resistance to parasites, situational awareness to aid in predation avoidance, and the ability to grow strong and healthy on natural forage. We'll reject any factory-farmed industrial breeds such as Cornish X chickens and broad-breasted white turkeys, opting instead for rare breeds that are more likely to thrive in a natural setting. These are breeds like American Chinchilla rabbits, Katahdin sheep and a slew of heritage turkey breeds; and breeds like the Ossabaw Island pig, a breed that has demonstrated it can make it on its own in a natural setting. The cows, sheep and rabbits should be able to thrive on the natural forages offered by our pastures. The pigs, however, since we must farm them at a higher stocking density than found in nature, will require supplemental feed.

The solution we conceived was an elegant one that required investment, learning a new skill, and consuming even more of our precious time. We chose to make those sacrifices in pursuit of the most biologically sustainable answer to the pig's growling tummies.

With heaps of confidence buoying a complete lack of experience, we reincarnated the dairy on George's land and learned to milk cows and make artisanal farmstead cheese.

All of this did nothing to impress the pigs—until they tasted the whey.

A Life Not Wasted
by Tim Young

From a Nature's Harmony Farm Blog Post, May 18, 2010

Last September, I blogged about the practice that many hatcheries have of grinding male chicks alive just after birth if they are of the laying breed variety. When people order a laying flock, understandably, they want females. You can read the blog post on our website, but as a quick recap, I mentioned that we take a different approach. That approach can be summarized as follows:

1. We value every life, whether it be a male "laying" chick or a male dairy calf.

2. The fact that some layers are born male instead of female presents an opportunity to us, not a problem for us.

3. We breed/incubate/hatch all of our own poultry. Otherwise, if we bought from hatcheries, we would be condoning and indeed supporting this wasteful practice.

4. In November, we hatched out over eight hundred layers, of which close to half could have been expected to be male.

5. We raise the males with the females in the eggmobiles and once they are of suitable size, process them as stewing birds.

Last Sunday was the first day of processing, as we harvested sixty roosters. We had so many interesting-looking roosters as there was all kinds of breeding going on between the breeds.

Since these roosters weren't of the meat breed variety, it took them about five months to grow to just over three pounds carcass weight, something your typical Cornish X could accomplish in about forty days. So they can't be looked at as a highly profitable farm enterprise, unless you sell them (and find someone to buy them) for three times the price of a typical meat chicken. We don't even try. We sell them for the cost of typical meat birds, and try to connect with consumers who understand what we're doing and support what we believe is the right solution to this problem. After all, while the bird may not be as young and tender, it makes up for that with (IMO) increased flavor and more interesting texture. It's the cook's job to figure out how to best use this gift, and we could probably all benefit from re-learning the art of cooking anyway.

These roosters have free ranged the pastures for recent months, and whereas some farmsteads have a single rooster to greet the sun, we have been serenaded with constant singing from here to there. Those voices are now starting to wane, but I am happy, very happy, that they had a shot at life as it was meant to be for them. It was a life not wasted.

CHAPTER 9

Agrarian Alchemy

A non-fiction fable featuring a seed, a farmer, a cow, and a cheese maker

In the vastness of nature is there anything less pretentious, less notable, less imposing, and yet so utterly full of hope and promise as a lone and humble seed? A miniscule seed that secretly harbors an ambition to become the tallest sequoia, the oldest olive tree or, perhaps, humbly aspires for no more than becoming watermeal, the smallest seed-bearing plant known to mankind. Watermeal is so small, in fact, that an estimated 5,000 plants are required to fill an everyday thimble![11]

And yet, the humble seed is a fair place to begin a magical journey of agrarian alchemy.

We begin our journey in a field of bare, freshly worked soil that has been liberated from decades of solar isolation and now embraces the sun's warmth for the first time in nearly twenty years. Having supplied moisture and nutrients for all that time to a dense, volunteer woodlot, it has waited patiently for this day. Now it is set free at last by a farmer whose aim is to increase available grazing land for his animals. He'll plant no grass seeds to do so, opting instead to take a ringside seat to observe one of many miracles of nature.

The soil, comprised of particles of broken rock weathered long and hard by Mother Nature and Father Time, also possesses a secret seed bank where seeds from time capsules long past await in dormancy.

An inconsequential seed can demonstrate remarkable forbearance, passing the days without complaint until a propitious event presents itself, allowing the seed to metamorphose into its destiny. In fact, in 1908, an Australian named A. J. Ewart germinated almost fifty examples of viable seeds that were older than fifty years, of which thirty-seven were legumes similar to clover. Indeed, later researchers reported similar findings, and found that pigweed and ragweed remain viable for over forty years in the soil, and some brassicas, such as mustard, remain viable for over fifty years![12]

For now the long wait is over and the soil, freshly cleared of dense, sun hogging forest canopy, is warmed and unleashes a remarkably heterogeneous array of photosynthetic life. Some of the new growth, such as pigweed, yellow nut sedge and mullein is undesirable by the farmer, but this matters not. Grazers, in the form of cows and sheep, are added to the land by the farmer, and quickly devour succulent, young growth that is to their liking. Depending on the time of year this may include millet, crabgrass, fescue, trefoil and hairy vetch.

As they trample the weedy plants that hold no interest for them the ruminants fertilize the new land, spreading seeds that pass through their digestive tracts intact. Seeds of forages grazed on pastures from which they were recently moved. In a few months, red and white clover, dallisgrass, chicory and other forages will be added to the forage mix on the cleared land, having been given a remarkable head start in one of nature's perfect incubators, the cow pie.

For this pasture reclamation project the farmer chose meat sheep and dairy cows, Jerseys, in particular. Thus every day at 4:00 p.m., the farmer walks his Jersey girls to the milking parlor a half-mile away to harvest their milk. Since his cows have consumed only grass, honoring their evolutionary heritage, the farmer will receive comparatively little milk, less than two gallons from each cow, which he will use to make cheese on farm. The volume of milk he receives seems absurdly low, indeed making him something of a laughingstock among commercial dairy farmers who enjoy prodigious volumes of milk, sometimes reaching more than ten gallons per cow, per day. He knows those hyper-inflated volumes are made possible by the feeding of high-energy grain—grain that he also knows cows did not evolve to consume, much less tolerate. Grain that requires prodigious amounts of labor and energy to grow, fertilize, weed, harvest and transport. Energy that, he reasons, can't have a positive impact on the earth's climate, and from reserves that will ultimately wither away.

As he walks the cows to the barn, nudging them along when they stop to nibble on grass, he wonders why all farmers don't just let the cows consume grass only. It's all about productivity and yield—everyone is chasing more, more, more! It makes sense to him anyway to let animals do the work of harvesting their own feed while fertilizing the land, rather than using metal and diesel in distant fields to grow, fertilize, weed, harvest, transport and then use labor to feed, when the cow is perfectly content feeding herself, freeing the farmer to kick back and watch. It's foolishness.

Still, the farmer has to sell his cheese and compete against other cheese makers, so the temptation is strong for him to give his cows just a little grain. Just enough, as other farmers are fond of saying, to get them into the milking parlor, even though he knows they need no prodding whatsoever to enter the parlor. Then maybe, *maybe,* he could get enough milk to make more cheese so that *maybe* he could compete and live a little more comfortably. Maybe.

He dismisses the thought, knowing this begins a slippery slope, for what constitutes a "little" grain? Would he then succumb to the temptation to feed more and then more, chasing higher yields the way methamphetamine addict's chase that illusive great high? Why stop there? Why not give antibiotics to keep animals healthy and milking longer?

When a customer looks at his cheese in the store and notices the price of his cheese is much higher, will they buy it, understanding that this reflects the real cost of producing food naturally and that the cheese is a much more nutritionally dense food since the cows only consumed organic pastures? Will the customer understand that this cheese was produced with no off-farm inputs and therefore has a positive environmental impact rather than detrimental? Will they care?

He knows the answer to these questions and he knows he'll receive few rewards for his sacrifices. Still he stands firm on his values. This farmer is chasing something more lasting than the short-term high other farmers chase by feeding grain and pumping up volume. He's chasing farming independence—complete, biological sustainability where he is dependent on nothing off the farm. If he can just get his cows, pigs, sheep, rabbits and other animals to thrive on what his land offers and nothing more then neither he nor they will require off-farm inputs. He's not there yet, but he's getting close.

In fact, learning the craft of cheese making allowed the farmer to solve two important problems, taking him that much closer to complete biological sustainability. The farmer wanted no soy in his animal feed and needed an alternative to buying feed for the slow-growing Ossabaw Island pigs that roamed his woodlots. It occurred to him that he could solve both problems by investing in a cheese making operation.

The idea was simple. Allow Jersey cows to graze organic pastures, make cheese from their raw milk, collect the whey as a by-product, and feed the whey back to the pigs. The whey would be a substantial feed source, as anywhere from 85% to 92% of the milk becomes whey in the cheese making process, depending on the type of cheese made and other variables. This would be one of many symbiotic, closed-loop systems on the farm. Cow eats grass, cow gives milk, milk becomes cheese to feed customers, whey becomes food for pigs instead of being a waste product, and pigs become pork for consumers. Actually, as he thought about it, the fat from the pigs would be made into lard which in turn would be used to coat the cheesecloth on the clothbound cheddar cheese he was about to make. To him it seemed to be a perfect closed-loop system! No, he would not feed grain. He's chasing something more lasting, something that will persist well after he's gone. He'll persevere.

When the milk has been collected the farmer dons his cheese-making cap and apron, prepares to warm the milk and make a batch of cheddar cheese, but not before he pours a taste of the milk, closes his eyes and embraces the flavors. In his mind, he sees the land where the cows grazed, tastes the clover and perhaps something else. Chicory? Minerals? He sets out to capture the flavor of the milk and nothing else by preserving the milk in the form of cheese. Unlike most producers, small or large, he doesn't pasteurize the milk, opting instead to make cheese from raw milk. This means that he won't be able to produce butter or fresh cheeses, as it's only legal to sell raw-milk cheeses that have aged for at least sixty days. In turn, this means at least sixty days of paying energy bills to keep the cooler running to age the cheese, and over a year in the case of the clothbound cheddar he'll make today. He tries to not think about this but he can't resist. Thoughts in his mind run amok once again, fighting one another as if there are several parties in his head having a fierce debate that no one can hear.

It's one thing that such low volumes of milk burden him, but he believes that using raw milk preserves nutritional qualities in the milk and allows for the real, unadulterated flavors of the milk to shine through. His penalty for wanting to preserve these nutritional and taste qualities is that he must pay to age the cheese at least sixty days and wait at least that long before he's paid a cent. Still, he aspires to pay homage to the milk and the tradition of cheese making by making the most flavorful and delicious cheese possible. A magnificent cheese! Why should he settle for anything less?

His family drinks only raw milk, of course, and the farmer makes delicious European-style cultured butter for personal use. At the end of today's cheese making process he'll save some deliciously salty and squeaky cheddar cheese curds that he'll enjoy with his wife in the evening. Customers would love to have these but, because they are made from raw milk, someone somewhere deems both to be a hazardous substance.

Hogwash!

Shaking his head, the farmer transfers the milk from the stainless bulk storage tank, which keeps the milk at about thirty-six degrees, to a 1,000-pound capacity stainless cheese vat, where it will be warmed and turned into cheese. The warming is accomplished by sending hot water through pipes that circulate in a jacket around the bottom of the vat. This allows the rate of temperature increase to be carefully controlled, a critical step in making cheddar cheese consistently well. As the milk warms from thirty-six degrees to ninety degrees, the cheese maker stirs the milk slowly and, relishing a brief moment unburdened by countless challenges on the farm, marvels at the rich, creamy froth as the temperature increases.

At lower temperatures white foam and small bubbles linger on the surface of the milk, giving the impression that the milk is comprised of many separate components rather than being a flowing, homogeneous fluid.

As the milk warms to around eighty degrees, the milk, now with a pronounced yellowish hue owing to the cow's diet of lush forage, kidnaps the cheese maker in a hypnotic trance, causing him to sway rhythmically as he gently stirs the milk.

His thoughts drift to the whole issue of raw milk, once again. It perplexes him to no end that consumers aren't allowed to decide for themselves if they want to buy and consume raw milk products, as their ancestors surely did. How in the world, he wonders, did they give up their freedom to do so? He knows the answer to this. Consumers didn't "give up" their freedom, it was simply and quietly taken away in 1987 as the Food and Drug Administration (FDA) began requiring milk to be pasteurized in the name of food safety. Well, at least the FDA didn't outlaw fast food, frozen pizzas, candy bars and high fructose corn syrup, all apparently deemed wholesome and safe by the same FDA.

The absurdity of this thought made the farmer chuckle audibly. The definition of "food" was being changed right before our collective eyes by forces beyond our perceived control, while we acquiesced from our sofas. Whereas food had historically been something anyone could harvest from the bounty of nature, such as berries from a plant, meat from an animal or milk from a cow, now virtually almost all "acceptable" foods were those that were processed and manufactured in cold, stainless steel factories. Historically we all had a right to procure food as we chose, but now that right is rapidly disappearing. The farmer's loyal customers include ardent supporters of what they label as real, nutrient-dense foods such as raw milk, and many are active members of the Weston A. Price foundation.

A native Canadian born in 1870, Dr. Weston A. Price became a prominent dentist and nutritional researcher in Cleveland, and is credited with at least fourteen publications between 1914-1939. His final publication was titled *Nutrition and Physical Degeneration: A Comparison of Primitive and Modern Diets and Their Effects*, and it is this publication that likely renewed interest in Dr. Price's research today. Indeed, the Weston A. Price foundation was co-founded in 1999 by Sally Fallon Morrel who authored the book *Nourishing Traditions: The Cookbook that Challenges Politically Correct Nutrition and the Diet Dictocrats*. It is Fallon's book that is often seen in the farmer's own kitchen and it is this book along with *The Omnivore's Dilemma* and *Animal, Vegetable, Miracle* that often sends customers on a winding path leading to his farm.

Dr. Price's final publication was fascinating though his writings were not without controversy in his time. In *Nutrition and Physical Degeneration,* Dr. Price set out to examine the health of many indigenous cultures and primitive races who did not benefit from, and therefore were unencumbered by, modern advancements in food manufacturing, health care and nutrition. He compared and contrasted numerous primitive and modern cultures, including Swiss, Polynesians, African Tribes, New Zealand Maori, Peruvian Indians, North American Indians and Australian Aborigines.

His research was thorough, but it was his photographs of native people that were most emotive. The photos vividly showed the teeth and facial structures of people exposed to a modern diet alongside their primitive counterparts, who were limited to a natural diet. Indeed, in some photographs, brothers were shown, each having lived his life in a different paradigm, one modern and one traditional. The comparisons were remarkable.

In Dr. Price's case a picture did tell a thousand words. The photographs of the "primitive's" dental and facial structure were captivating. Page after page of naturally beautiful, happy people with perfect teeth, most living in villages with no physician of any kind, including a dentist. By contrast, photographs of those with access to modern diets and health care showed severe dental disease. Beyond the photographs, Dr. Price found remarkable differences in the effect of other illnesses and disease among proximate populations whose only significant difference was in their diet and exposure to modern health care. A clear example of these findings was illustrated by Dr. Price's comparison of isolated and modernized Swiss populations.

With assistance from the Swiss government, a group of two thousand people were identified for study in 1931 and 1932. This group, located in the Loetschental Valley, lived in a physical environment that made access to modern food or health care virtually impossible. People had lived in this valley for over twelve hundred years and had never been conquered, owing in part to three high mountain ranges, usually snow-capped, in which their valley was comfortably nestled. Passage in and out of the valley is possible via or alongside a river that descends to the Rhone Valley, and locals, who could trigger artificial landslides and trap the intruders, easily guarded the passage against attack. Moreover, according to Dr. Price's writings, natural landslides make passage treacherous or impossible for most of the year, and it is this reason that necessitated the valley inhabitants to find ways to survive, and thrive, on their own.

Dr. Price found that the valley inhabitants had no physician and no dentist. They made their own clothes of wool from their sheep and the valley provided everything they needed for both clothing and food, with a possible and singular exception being sea salt. They used no horses, no trucks, wagons, tractors or mechanical equipment, relying instead on the strength of their hearts and backs to move up and down mountain terrain.

Dr. Price studied adults and growing girls and boys, as well as samples of food. Since virtually every household had goats, cows or both, he also studied dairy products closely throughout 1931. The samples tested were found to be high in vitamins and much higher than average commercial samples found in America, Europe and lower Switzerland. While a limited amount of garden vegetables were grown for summer use, milk, cheese and butter were stored to comprise a large portion of the diet for the year, along with rye. Meat, from animals that were obviously raised naturally eating forages they evolved to eat, was enjoyed about once per week. This diet included fat and organs from the animals along with muscle tissue.

Dr. Price found fourteen cultures in all that exhibited the superb good health of the Swiss villagers. These cultures were located in different parts of the world—from the frozen north, to the tropics to the high mountains of South America. The particulars of each diet were different, but the main underlying characteristic of every healthy diet was the high levels of vitamins and minerals in the diets. The diets were found to be at least four times richer in minerals—calcium, phosphorus, iron, magnesium, iodine, etc.—and ten times richer in what Dr. Price called the "fat-soluble activators," the vitamins A, D and K_2. In the case of the Swiss villagers, these would have mainly been derived from organ meats, fats and butterfat of grassfed animals, but other cultures derived these same vitamins from certain seafood, such as fish eggs, shellfish and fish liver oil.

First described by Dr. Price in 1945 as a "vitamin-like activator," vitamin K_2 is produced either by animals eating green grass or by marine life with diets based on plankton; it is necessary for the development of wide facial bones, the same facial bones that glowed so healthily in his vivid photographs. For Westerners today, the most acceptable sources of this vital nutrient are whole cheese and butter from grass-fed cows.

So what were his findings in the Swiss study? Of the children in the valley following this primitive diet, the average number of cavities per person was 0.3. In other words, Dr. Price had to examine, on average, *three* children to find even *one* defective tooth. Moreover, even though tuberculosis was the most serious disease of Switzerland at the time, not one death from tuberculosis had ever been reported in the valley.

So it's not surprising that, like many of his customers, the farmer embraced Dr. Price's findings as something that just plain made sense. The healthiest people were the ones who lived the most natural lives and consumed diets free of chemicals and processed foods. He wondered if most of his customers fully understood that they now are not allowed to partake in something that was such a fundamental part of daily life for each of their ancestors? How on earth could the government deem it safe for so many processed foods with so many unpronounceable, manufactured by-product ingredients to be sold legally, and yet label fresh raw milk, long considered as wholesome and natural as any food, as harmful and illegal?

How would the farmer explain to a child that, once they're older, they would earn the right to buy alcohol, guns and cigarettes, but not milk? Congratulations young man, have a smoke.

"Is the milk more dangerous even than the cigarettes Mr. Farmer?" the child may ask.

The cheese maker snaps out of his daze, infuriated that his lips have been moving while he carried on this silent rant with no one. Realizing that he is now holding the stirring paddle so tightly that his wrists throb, he exhales deeply and calms himself. His gaze returns to the vat and his attention to the task in front of him—making cheese.

Thick, creamy and moving with glacial speed, the milk now looks much different, evoking delightful images of a viscous river of softened ice cream. The farmer and his fury retire to the background, supplanted by the cheese maker who is, once again, lulled into the moment at hand. And it is at this precise moment that the farmer, now morphed into cheese maker, realizes that there is no place on earth that he would rather be.

With the target temperature achieved, the cheese maker adds a mixture of starter cultures to the milk. The cultures are mainly bacteria, whose mission is to eat the milk sugars, otherwise known as lactose, and expel lactic acid. The result of this is that the pH will drop gradually during the next hour and then sharply for many hours after the curds are cut, so the cheese maker records the pH of the milk and logs it.

The cheese maker lets the bacteria munch on the lactose for about an hour, giving him some time to clean and sanitize the cheese room, a job that knows no end. When the time is right, the cheese maker adds rennet to the milk, marking the point for most people where the alchemy begins. The rennet will help the milk to coagulate, resulting in a firm curd, thus turning the liquid into a solid.

Rennet is an enzyme, or group of enzymes, that is produced in the stomach of young mammals and aids in the digestion of their mother's milk. Rennet, and therefore cheese making, was a stroke of serendipity, as some long-ago ancestor likely used a calf's stomach to store and transport his milk. The next day, he would have observed that the milk had curdled, separating into solid chunks of curd bobbing in liquid whey. The intrepid soul may have munched on what he must have presumed was solid milk but at some point figured that the curds could be separated, dried, salted and, if desired, pressed. This landmark discovery would have earned him great admiration as he alone could then transform milk from a highly perishable food into cheese, a preserved and easily transportable food. In his time, truly this metamorphosis would have bordered on alchemy.

Later, his descendants would learn that it was in the lining of the last of the ruminant's four stomachs, the abomasum, and in particular the enzyme chymosin, that caused the curdling. This began a tradition of slicing the calf's abomasum into strips, salting and drying each strip to be used for later cheese making.[13]

This approach works as well today as it did millennia ago, but today's cheese maker has five categories of choices to consider when selecting rennet.

The first category is traditional animal rennet, which is extracted from the abomasum of a young milk-fed calf. This is the method favored for thousands of years to make the cheeses so many people have grown to love. Cheeses like cheddar, Gruyere, Gouda, and Brie. If you're curious how the rennet is extracted from the young calf the answer is not complicated. The calf is simply killed and his stomach removed. Today this often occurs as a "by-product" of slaughtering young veal calves who have been milk-fed and virtually immobilized for their short, tightly confined lives—if that's what their existence can be called. Frequently raised in a wooden crate that measures only fifty-four inches by twenty-two inches, and never seeing either the sun or its mother, the calf can't walk or turn around by design, thus ensuring that his muscles atrophy so the diner can enjoy tender veal.[14]

With his commitment to raising animals in natural settings the farmer is understandably quite disturbed by this notion. Of course there is a market for it but the farmer firmly refuses to produce veal. Indeed, one of his farming tenets is that all of his animals must have the opportunity to reach maturity before their ultimate harvest date. This is why he raises slow-growing heritage meat chickens for a minimum of eighty-four days instead of the thirty-nine sought by industrial farmers. There is no way in good conscience that he can condone the use of animal rennet despite the fact that it honors tradition and he lets the cheese maker know it. The cheese maker seeks an alternative.

For obvious reasons, animal rights activists and vegetarians are uncomfortable with animal-based rennet, and there are two categories of choices that they favor if they hope to enjoy cheese. One is microbial rennet that is derived from a mold, yeast or fungus, and grown in a lab. This type of rennet may be satisfactory to overcome moral objections, but most professional cheese makers believe its use results in bitterness, particularly as a cheese ages.

Another option for vegetarians is pure vegetable-based rennet derived from plants such as fig tree bark, cardoon thistle, and nettles, which produce the necessary coagulating enzymes. Again, however, these types of rennet often impart bitterness and are less predictable than other forms of rennet. Their origins satisfy the farmer but not the cheese maker, as they do not allow him to make the aged cheeses he aspires to create and that his customers will want to enjoy.

Of course another coagulating alternative is simply citric acid, lemon juice, or vinegar, and these are sometimes used in making young, cooked cheeses. In aged cheeses, which the cheese maker is forced to make due to federal laws mandating long aging of cheeses from raw milk, young cheeses are not legal and use of vinegar will introduce a noticeable and undesirable flavor profile.

It is this fact that entices the cheese maker to examine one additional category of rennet.

Thanks to modern technology, fermentation-produced chymosin (FPC), a genetically engineered coagulant identical in nature to calf chymosin, is now produced and widely used. The manufacturing process for FPC includes extracting the gene that is responsible for the chymosin enzyme from the abomasum and marrying it to a host microorganism. The result is a form of coagulant that allows cheese to be produced and aged consistent with an old-world technique and flavor profile. This is what the cheese maker is after.

Of course there's a down side as the pertinacious farmer who now storms to the cerebral foreground is only too eager to point out. FPC is obviously a product of genetically modified organisms (GMO), a practice that the farmer strictly frowns upon and he firmly lets the cheese maker know it. The cheese maker, in a bit of an "ah ha" moment, counters that it is true that FPC is a product of GMO technology but that it doesn't itself contain any living genetically engineered organisms. This, continues the cheese maker, makes it akin to the same category of substances as human insulin, which is used by so many to treat diabetes. It's not at all the same as genetically engineered seeds promulgated by Monsanto, knowing full well that this agri-behemoth is a favorite villain of the farmer.

The farmer in his overalls stares sternly in the mirror at the cheese maker in his apron, neither yielding. Fuming, they're both thinking the same thing. Why should the simple process of converting milk into cheese be fraught with so many complex choices—to sacrifice an animal simply for his stomach, to use molds and vegetables to make an unpalatable cheese, or to save the animal and make a delicious cheese but surrender to technological advancements with far-reaching ramifications?

The stare down continues, until after moments of fuming the farmer's eyes drop in capitulation to a riddle without a "right" answer. He walks away in defeat and defers to the cheese maker.

The cheese maker opts decisively for FPC, acknowledging that, while it is not perfect, represents the best of the choices for his needs. The discussion over, the matter concluded, the farmer retires to the background and the cheese maker resumes his business.

Another hour has passed and the cheese maker suspects it is time to cut the curds. To confirm his suspicion he checks for a clean break by simply inserting a knife into the jelly-like coagulum, and slowly lifts it to see if the mass breaks cleanly. It does, and the cheese harps are removed from the sanitizer in the sink. The cheese maker now cuts the curds.

The first harp is used to cut horizontal layers in the coagulum. It is pulled very gently and slowly by the gentle hands of the cheese maker, the same hands that the farmer used the day before with great force to remove and repair a 250-pound tractor tire. The cheese maker knows that it is important to handle the curds very gently for the next few minutes as they will release too much whey if they are handled too aggressively when the mass is first cut. Among other things this will result in reduced yield, something that can scarcely be afforded given the already low volume of milk available.

The goal of cutting the curds is to expel whey and separate liquid from solids. By cutting the curds into small particles the cheese maker greatly multiplies the available surface area exposed, thus making it much easier, and faster, for whey to escape. With the horizontal layer now cut the cheese maker slowly pulls the harp with vertical wires through the vat, cutting the curds into smaller pieces.

If he were making a young, high-moisture cheese, such as Camembert or Brie, the cheese maker would be content simply cutting long ribbons or curd particles at least one half inch or greater in size. By contrast, if he were making a cooked cheese such as Gruyere, one of his favorites, he would cut the curds multiple times until they were but the size of grains of rice, allowing them to quickly expel whey and firm up.

The original makers of Gruyere had reason indeed to ensure as much moisture as possible was removed from the cheese. The process for making Gruyere evolved as a sensible means of preserving the summer milk high in the Swiss Alps. As temperatures warmed and snow melted on the mountains, cows from villages below would migrate far up the mountainsides in chase of lush forages, bringing farmers and portable milking stations behind them. To preserve the milk, cheese makers followed the trail and set up portable cheese-making facilities on the mountain, where they were charged with preserving the milk in such a manner that it would not only last through the winter, but so that it could be easily transported back to the villages when the autumn snows forced descent. Such a challenge was daunting, made even more so by the fact that salt was rare, owing to their distance from the sea.

The solution was to make a low-moisture, firm cheese by expelling as much whey as possible. Cheese makers learned to accomplish this by cutting the curd pieces as small as possible and by cooking the cheese at temperatures up to 130 degrees over a fire in a copper kettle. Once the curds were cooked, stirred and achieved a bouncy texture when tested by the cheese maker, they were removed and placed in large round cheese molds where they were pressed to remove any additional whey. The finished wheels, measuring perhaps four inches tall, would weigh eighty-five pounds or more and literally, if desired, could be rolled down hills. When stored in the right conditions these low-moisture cheeses would not only last a year or more, they would get better every day.

Today the cheese maker is making cheddar, not Gruyere, and so he doesn't cut the curds as aggressively. He opts for a 3/8-inch curd particle, something he doesn't literally measure, but eyes as a curd size between that of blue cheese and Gruyere. With the curds now cut, he allows them to settle in the vat for a few minutes, and notes the temperature of the whey, which remains at ninety degrees. Now, he turns the hot water back on and begins the process of carefully increasing the temperature of the curds and whey to 102 degrees.

In making cheddar the temperature increase must be achieved slowly and carefully. Otherwise too much whey may be expelled, the curds may be overcooked and the desired outcome won't be achieved. A slow and meticulous process, the cheese maker aims to only increase the temperature one degree every four minutes. The cerebral calculator flips on in his head as he mumbles to himself while stirring.

"It's 90 degrees now and I want to go to 102, so that's an increase of twelve degrees. I want my rate of increase to be one degree every four minutes, so that's four minutes times twelve degrees. Forty-eight minutes. It's 9:35 a.m. now, so I should be at my target temperature at 10:18—no, 10:23 a.m. The halfway point will be at about 10:00 a.m., so I should be at 96 degrees then."

There's no button to push, not automatic system to accomplish this delicate rise in temperature for him. He simply adjusts the rate of flow of the hot water entering the jacketed vat, stirs and keeps an excruciatingly close eye on the thermometer. If it starts rising too fast, he'll reduce the water flow. Too slow and he'll increase. He's done this a few times before by now, so he has developed a pretty good feel for it.

He reaches the target temperature at 10:26 a.m., a little late, but close enough. The water is turned off and the curds are cooked at this temperature until the pH drops to 6.0 or so and the curd pellets achieve a certain springiness when handled. On this day, it takes almost two hours to achieve the target pH, but once attained, he takes a large board and pushes the curds to the back of the vat and holds them there. Just then in a distant woodlot, the pigs prepare for supper as the cheese maker drains the whey from the vat, fills a dozen five-gallon buckets and summons the farmer.

Feeding the whey to the pigs is always a fun, albeit challenging task, as the pigs run over the farmer in pursuit of the whey. It's not clear who is the happier recipient of this form of alchemy, the pigs who receive the whey or the customers who receive the cheese, but all the same there's no waste.

With the whey now drained a curd mass has been formed in the back of the vat, approximately eight inches deep, and the cheese maker now begins what is called the cheddaring process. A trench is cut in the middle so that whey can begin to drain off, and within a few minutes, the cheese maker cuts the mass into slabs that are about six inches wide by eight inches tall. He waits fifteen minutes, and then flips each slab, but also starts the process of stacking them on top of one another. Fifteen minutes later, he unstacks and flips all slabs, then stacks them three high. This process repeats itself until a pH of 5.4 or so is recorded, all the while ensuring that the curds stay at a temperature of ninety-five to one hundred degrees.

Once the desired pH is observed, the curds are milled, or cut back into small pieces. Commercial operations use cheddar mills for this, which act something like sausage grinders. Our farmstead cheese maker, having not the resources or interest in such highfalutin devices, simply uses a hand-operated French fry cutter. One by one he hand cuts chunks of curd masses that will fit in his flimsy cutter where he can then cut ribbons the size and shape of French fries.

As he finishes with the cutting, he prepares to salt liberally, applying about three percent of the weight of the curds in salt. As he does this, he thinks about how cheddar making must have evolved compared to other firm cheeses such as Gruyere. Whereas salt was scarce in the Alps it would have been abundant in Britain. Thus when devising a means for transporting preserved milk from the countryside to the burgeoning population in London, the cheese makers could use salt liberally to further draw out whey, both flavoring the cheese and creating a lower moisture environment, robbing harmful bacteria of much of the hospitable environment they desired. This thought fascinated the cheese maker, as both Gruyere and cheddar may be perceived in a similar fashion when feeling or looking at a wheel, but the process that evolved to produce the cheeses is vastly different. It is these old-world methods that the cheese maker aspires to learn, master and pass on.

With the curds salted the cheese maker prepares the molds he himself made, lines them with cheese cloth that has been soaking in whey, tightens a strap around the outside and fills each with curds. Once they will hold no more, he pulls the cheesecloth over the top as if tucking in a baby for the night. Indeed these are his babies.

He stacks the hoops one on top of the other, today having made only three. Each will end up weighing about thirteen pounds, a far cry from the thirty-five- to forty-pound wheels most cheese makers make. Then again most cheddar cheese makers have expensive hydraulic cheese presses that can generate the force to press those cheeses. Cheddar is pressed at a far greater rate of pressure than Gruyere, hence the need for hydraulic presses. Our humble cheese maker takes a different approach, placing a board on top of the cheeses and pressing with five-gallon buckets filled with water. He's not sure what amount of pressure per square inch he's using. The experts say he's supposed to know but he figures the cheese was made quite well long ago without such knowledge, and so he pays attention to what he's doing, observes the outcome and develops a feel for it. His feel. His cheese.

The next day after the cheeses have been pressed he prepares for the final step. The cheeses are removed from the molds, allowed to air dry for a while, and then are wrapped in fresh cheese cloth. Then the cheese maker takes lard made by the farmer's wife from the fat of an Ossabaw Island pig, melts it, and brushes it all over the cheesecloth, sealing in moisture and sealing out as much as he can. He takes the cheeses to his temperature-controlled cave where they will remain at fifty-two degrees and 90% humidity for twelve months. Twelve months until he will be paid, twelve months of utility bills and twelve months of hand-brushing and caring for the cheese. He knows he could do much better financially by simply making young, bloomy rind cheeses like Camembert, but to him, this cheese is worth the wait.

With the cheese now tucked away and the cheese room cleaned, the cheese maker turns off the lights and leaves the building, where he is greeted once again by the farmer. This time the farmer has a kind word for the cheese maker and congratulates him for his role in completing a remarkable form of agrarian alchemy. The cleared land contributed the nutrients, the rain moistened the ground allowing the dormant seeds in the seed bank to germinate and harvest solar energy, thus the seeds became the grass, the grass, with assistance from the cow became the milk, the milk became the cheese, the whey fed the pigs and both the pigs and the cheese nourished us, the humans. The circle was complete, the inputs were few and the waste was non-existent, as in the case with nature.

Exhausted but contently fulfilled, the farmer and cheese maker retire for the evening, thinking not of what tomorrow will bring but of what they accomplished today.

Today, if for one day only, they were agrarian wizards.

CHANGING PRIORITIES IN ORDER TO FARM
BY LIZ YOUNG

From a Nature's Harmony Farm Blog Post, July 14, 2009

We've been extremely fortunate to get a good bit of media attention about what we are doing on our farm. The only thing to which I can attribute this interest is that people are talking more and more about local and sustainable food and so more reporters are looking to tell the story. We are always thankful when they offer to use our farm as an example because we feel that any attention that can be brought to sustainable farming is positive. Yes, we understand the arguments from vegetarians and the people who feel that small-scale farmers cannot feed the world, but we believe strongly in what we are doing and it is a passion that is leading our lives.

One of the things that I do find disappointing, however, is when people assume that it takes a lot of money to farm this way and to eat this type of food. I've been reflecting lately on our priorities and I'm just not convinced that things are as expensive as some are led to believe. Yes, Tim and I both had stable income for years, which afforded us the ability to buy a nice home in the suburbs. This is not that atypical, though. The difference for us was that we decided to trade assets. When we decided that we wanted land to farm, we also made the decision that we had to move out to the rural country in

211

order to afford land. As a result we are over two hours away from Atlanta, in a place where we are lucky just to be able to get good cell phone coverage. This lifestyle has led us down a path of trading in many other priorities, such as no more vacations, no more dining out, no new cars, or no new clothes. The daily living expenses that we used to incur have just been allocated elsewhere in order to buy seeds for the garden and invest in tractors and livestock.

Farming has not made us poor, nor will it make us rich, but in the end our only goal is to sustain. When we made a change in our lifestyle, we also changed the things we value. We have no desire for many of the pastimes we used to have. Our vacation is sitting in the pasture with the cows or fishing in the pond. Our nice dinners out are when we can take a couple of hours to make a four-course meal in the comfort of our own home. And new clothes? Forget about it! I just try not to have too much dirt under my nails! I guess my point is that the last thing I want to see happen is for future farmers to feel discouraged because they don't have enough money to take the leap into farming. When you are willing to dedicate your life to this you will find a way to make it work.

Another daunting thought that most farmers feel is, "How will I get customers?" All I can say is that I am constantly amazed at what our customers do to demonstrate their priorities. For the people who believe that eating this way is beyond their budget because they are comparing chicken at $1.50/lb. at the grocery store to Poulet Rouge at $4.50/lb., I offer you a few examples of inspiration.

At the farmers' market this weekend a new customer came to our booth with a big smile and said that they were so happy to finally be able to get to the market. They said for some time they had wanted to buy food from our farm, but could never get a Saturday off work to get to the market. They were able to make this particular Saturday because they had lost their job just three days prior. They bought five pounds of ground beef and a dozen eggs and said they would definitely see us again in the future.

How can they buy this "expensive" food at a time like that? Priorities.

Another couple who have been great customers of ours for some time have been sharing their story of a long, drawn-out company closing. For months they have been facing the fact that they will lose half of their family's income, yet they have sworn to us that they are so dedicated to buying healthy food that they made plans to cut expenses in other areas in order to continue to support sustainable farming. They will give up cable, home phone, and the Internet before they give up their nutrition. It's a choice of priorities.

I met a customer last month who called because she likes to support local food but was having a hard time finding a good supplier. She apologized in advance for having some weird questions then went on to ask about organ meats and the specifics of our animal's diets. She explained that some time ago, in order to save money she made a drastic change to the way she eats. She now feeds her family a variety of "cheap cuts" that most people overlook. She put together an order of many pounds of food consisting of liver, spleen, fat, kidney, and ground beef—all for less than forty dollars. She changed her tastes to meet her priorities.

Our customers come from all walks of life. They are young and old, well-off and struggling. Some have very large families to feed and others use our food only on special occasions. The point is that this is not only for the rich; it is for those who prioritize healthy, naturally raised food over other discretionary spending.

Most customers come to the realization that it wasn't as expensive as they originally thought. They tell us how the food is so flavorful and satisfying that they find they eat smaller portions. They also share how they are extending each cut to make many meals, as one of our great customers wrote on her blog when a single chicken fed them for thirteen meals. After an initial thought of it being costly, they realized that it boiled down to $1.38 per meal!

So, I believe it's a cop-out to say that organic farming and food is expensive. It's extremely challenging and lots of hard work for both the farmer and consumer to have food this way, but when it becomes your priorities you realize that you do in fact have a choice. Our choice was to farm. We don't feel like we gave up anything at all. Rather, our lives are richer than ever.

CHAPTER 10

Downshifting

During tours of Nature's Harmony Farm we're often asked the question, "Can you make money farming?" What a bizarre question that is! In what other profession is this question asked with such frequency, innocence and curiosity?

"Pardon me, doctor, but while you're taking out my appendix, I'm curious—can you make money being a doctor?"

I never thought to ask anyone such a question. You probably haven't either. Was I sometimes curious? Perhaps, but I wouldn't ask. Yet it is among the most frequent questions we receive, sometimes tactfully disguised and sometimes an outright "How much money do you make?"

Making money is not a term that has a lot of agricultural relevance in my view. I would argue that it's not even in itself a worthy goal. After all, why do we want to "make money" in the first place? Presumably the answer relates to security. That is to say, freedom and independence. Farming, particularly diversified, biologically sustainable farming, is an occupation unlike any other. It should go without saying that first on our collective list of priorities in life are water and sustenance. Only after these needs are satisfied do comfort, security and higher aspirations even warrant consideration. Yet only one occupation can fulfill our most basic human needs, and that is producing your own sustenance through farming. If you can accomplish this on your own you indeed will have a lot of security, which begs the question—how much additional money do you need?

Part of the answer to that question will depend on how you prioritize things. When someone asks if you can make money, what are they asking? Are they asking if they can "clear" a certain amount of money each year? If so, how much are they seeking? A hundred dollars? A hundred thousand dollars? Are they simply concerned with meeting their modest tax, utility and basic living expenses and nothing more? Or do they wish to fund whatever discretionary expenses they desire, such as satellite TV, travel, fine dining, luxuries and frequent automobile purchases? There is nothing wrong with wanting these things, but perhaps you can see how not knowing the answer makes it challenging for us. We don't know, so we can't answer.

Perhaps they're not concerned with how much they clear but rather they are simply concerned with wealth accumulation. The two are quite different. For example, take the local dairy farmers I know who for much of 2009-2010 were losing money on each cow. Given the collapsing price of milk for a lengthy period of time, they had to go to the bank repeatedly to borrow money to cover feed bills. I can assure you that even though the prices of wholesale milk plummeted the price of feed did no such thing.

Why would a farmer endure losses day in and day out on their dairy operation? Moreover, why would the bank lend them money to do so? The answer lies in the wealth of their assets along with the projected growth of that wealth, or what the bank would refer to as collateral.

I'll try to illustrate what I mean.

Let's say that a dairyman owns a dairy with one hundred cows. He's fortunate enough to have inherited this land from his family. Thus while he has no mortgage, he must pay taxes and expenses that accompany operating the dairy.

Most commercial dairies feed a dairy ration of grain to their cows. On average this may be thirty to fifty pounds or more *per day per cow*. This results in astonishing volumes of milk produced, reaching up to fifteen gallons per day per cow, although seven gallons per day is closer to the average. Of course, there is the cost of feed to produce this, but the farmer wouldn't routinely incur that expense if the compensation didn't justify it.

However, for the sake of this example let's assume that dairy cows are managed the way we do at Nature's Harmony Farm, where their only feed intake is in the form of grass. Feeding one hundred dairy cows only grass would require a sizable farm, with at least a hundred acres of well-managed pasture. While this would result in an embarrassingly low milk output of maybe two gallons per day per cow, there would be the benefit of no feed costs. So the only costs would be chemicals for cleaning the pipeline milking system, minor repairs, utilities to operate the dairy, and labor—but only if the dairy farmer chose to hire a part-time helper, which he wouldn't have to. If he elected to use veterinarians, there would of course be an occasional cost for that.

Most dairies milk each cow for about ten months before drying her off before her next lactation cycle. So each cow is milked for approximately three hundred days per year. At two gallons per day in a grass-fed model he could reasonably expect six hundred gallons per cow, per year.

Over a recent fifteen-year period, milk prices paid to the dairy farmer averaged $13.64/CWT. The "CWT" stands for hundredweight, meaning the farmer was paid $13.64 for every one hundred pounds of milk. A gallon of milk is calculated to weigh 8.6 pounds, resulting in 11.63 gallons per hundred pounds. Thus, a farmer earned, on average for the fifteen-year period, $1.17 per gallon ($13.64/11.63).

Given those prices an economic value of $702 could be attributed to the typical cow that contributed six hundred gallons to the farm. A simple calculation would disclose that the farmer would earn $70,200 in gross revenue during the year for the one hundred cows in the herd and still enjoy, along with the cows, two months off.

Now keep in mind that these are *wholesale* numbers. If the farmer elects to sell direct to customers the income potential (and the workload) is far greater. As of this writing, the lowest price that I know of for raw milk produced from grass-fed cows is about $8/gallon, but that's if you can find it anywhere. Consumers are learning more about how their food is produced and they are becoming increasingly connected to its origin, as well as becoming disenchanted with factory farming and processed foods. Yet most people still compartmentalize things in their mind and think, for example, that all raw milk is the same. In reality, virtually every dairy feeds anywhere from a little to a lot of grain to their cows to increase milk production, as previously mentioned. While more milk may flow, it is milk fueled largely by grain and there is an increasing body of research that shows substantial nutritional benefits to consuming meat and dairy from cows that are grass-fed *only*.

Allowing cows access only to the forages they evolved to eat makes perfect sense to me, but it's unlikely you'll see too many conventional dairies making the switch. A big reason is because they would need to concentrate on pasture management, ensuring that adequate forage is available virtually year 'round. Whereas cows can literally be raised on cement (and indeed are in many cases) when feed is placed in troughs in front of them, grass-fed operations can only raise as many animals as the land will allow. This represents a double whammy for most dairy farmers as they would not only see a substantial decline in the milk output per cow once the high-energy ration was removed, they would also have to make do with far fewer cows. Given that consumers don't normally know (or question) the difference between grass-fed and non grass-fed raw milk, there's little incentive to make the switch.

However, for the rare farmer who does produce grass-fed raw milk at $8/gallon, each cow would generate a whopping $4,800 per year! Of course the farmer then has a host of additional burdens including marketing (to find the customers), purchasing and maintaining bottling equipment, bottling supplies, labor for bottling and delivery, fuel costs, coolers for storage, spoilage, product liability insurance, payment management, and so on.

So what is the answer? Would the farm be profitable or not? The answer depends on the costs to operate the dairy, which should indeed be far below the revenue earned, along with the living expenses required by the owner, which, depending on their needs, is highly situational. Thus far, this illustration only addresses what is considered to be the profitability, or cash flow, part of the equation. What about wealth accumulation?

Let's assume that each of the one hundred cows will produce one calf per year and that half of those will be females. (The reality is that for most dairies today far more than half will be females, as dairy geneticists have learned much about sex selection with bull semen. Yes, you can order, at an additional expense, semen that has a high likelihood of producing a female calf. After all, the bull calf has a very short life in a dairy.)

So after the winter vacation and the cows and their farmer are rested, fifty female calves will be born. These calves, on good dairies, could be sold within a year at a minimum of $1,000 each but on better dairies up to $2,000 each. So at $1,000 each let's add a minimum of $50,000 to the $70,200 in milk income for an annual income of $120,200. The bull calves would go for much less, but may fetch $200 each, so let's add $10,000 for that.

Perhaps the farmer wishes to keep all of his female calves as what is referred to as replacement heifers. They will be bred when they are over one year old, most likely to calve at twenty-four months of age. At this time, they will begin producing milk and will replace (hence the term "replacement heifer") one of the older milk cows, or be an addition to the herd. If they are a replacement, the older cow will be sold at an auction for, perhaps, $.75/lb., or $800-$1,000. However, if the farmer has the land and forage available to increase his herd size from one hundred to one hundred fifty, then his income would increase linearly. His cleaning costs would remain unchanged as he cleans the milking system once regardless of whether he milks ten cows or hundred, but his income increases from $70,200 to $105,300.

That doesn't sound quite as good as it did if he sold the fifty female calves and earned $120,200 during the year, does it? Ah, but let's not forget that he now owns 150 milk cows instead of one hundred, who not only have a minimum market value of $150,000 and will produce seventy-five female calves the next year, but will, at virtually no cost, *continue* producing milk and calves. Year after year. For him, it is literally a "cash cow." So the dairy farmer, with his perpetual production plant, accumulates assets and a cash flow engine even though he may lose money in the short term.

Of course, you may be thinking that this farmer is lucky to own the hundred acres of pasture, and perhaps you're not so lucky. So what about you? In many areas, farmland can be purchased for about $3,000 per acre. At an interest rate of five pecent, the annual cost to service the mortgage on the land would be just over $22,000 per year, far less than the $120,200 the farmer brings in. Granted, a new farmer would still have to procure dairy cows and set up the dairy, but perhaps this can help you to better understand the profit implications, and risks, of one particular farming enterprise. It requires capital, risk assumption, making decisions about how to go to market (wholesale/direct), industry knowledge and solid execution. These same success factors apply to any and every business. And like any other business, it can be executed either highly successfully or catastrophically unsuccessfully.

So I ask you—is this farmer profitable?

You decide.

In our case, once we moved to the country and chose to become farmers we realized that wouldn't be able to both farm *and* continue living the way we had been accustomed. It was clear that something would have to change and that "something" was our priorities.

In retrospect, changing priorities wasn't as difficult for us as one might think. We had so clearly articulated the values that we held dear that we did not feel like we were sacrificing. Then again I suppose one could say we have. It's simply a matter of perspective. It is true that we gave up buying nice clothes and indeed almost never buy any new clothes. We have no interest in buying at Kohl's or Banana Republic when we can get something much better, for a farmer, at Goodwill, the ultimate recycling store. And save a bundle too!

Vacations? Where would we want to go? We're already there. We moved here to have a permanent vacation. When Liz and I want to get away, we take a long, leisurely pasture walk around the perimeter of the farm. Meandering in and out of woodlots, past one of two ponds, we can walk for miles and miles and never leave the property. We stop and greet the pigs in each of their five paddocks, visit cows, sheep, donkeys, turkeys, chickens, peacocks, rabbits, and guineas, enjoying occasional repose when a view captivates us, as it does at every turn. If we really do want to get away we've found that our ideal getaways now mirror our life. No longer do we long for Las Vegas, Amsterdam or St. Thomas. Two days of camping at an expense of, maybe, thirty bucks a day all-in is our idea of paradise. Perched by a stream with a small campfire we are connected with nature but removed from the responsibilities of the farm. And yet the farm beckons in a very good way and steers us home. We can't stand to be separated for very long.

Now it is also true that there are but a handful of exquisite restaurants within an hour of the farm. Still, one sacrifice that wasn't required was enjoying five-star dinners with unsurpassed views. On any night we choose our dinner may begin on an outdoor patio overlooking impossibly green fields dotted with contently grazing animals, rippling ponds and the serenade of nearby peacocks, roosters and guineas. The first course may include an aged organic, raw milk cheese—let's see, tonight it will be a blue cheese accompanied by a sixteen-month-old Gruyere. I made both on the farm from our Jersey cow's raw milk. Honey that Liz harvested from our beehives is drizzled over the blue, creating a delectable sweet/salty contrast. The bread that Liz made is from wheat that she ground, which I planted and grew. It is still warm, and is a waiting bed for the fresh butter that she also made from the gift of cream from our Jersey cows.

It's a beautiful April evening so we go outside to enjoy this appetizer with a glass of Cabernet Sauvignon from our first vintage. The fact that grape vines are inexpensive allowed us to plant a hundred of them so that we could enjoy truly local, organic wine while not giving up on life's pleasures. It's not the best Cabernet I've ever had by any stretch, but it's mine. Some people may believe that you need to sacrifice to the point of deprivation in order to farm. We don't. We simply prioritized and redefined our values.

As we sip the wine and enjoy the appetizers we laugh and watch baby lambs hop, run and play through the pasture. It's the same rerun every year—baby lambs, until they're about a month old, start hopping and dancing convulsively every day as dusk approaches. It's only at that time of day and only at that age. Then, virtually overnight, they outgrow it. Today they haven't and we soak it all in. Life is beautiful.

I kiss Liz on the forehead and walk over to the grill to check on the organic grass-fed filet mignon steaks that are wrapped in bacon, which I made, from our rare Ossabaw Island hogs. As I flip the steaks it occurs to me that this may be the only place in the world where you can get this combination. Asparagus from our garden is in season now and has cozied up next to the steaks on the grill. I am reminded how we used to buy cardboard-like asparagus year 'round before reading what is now one of my favorite books, *Animal, Vegetable, Miracle,* by Barbara Kingsolver. Before farming we were not in touch with the seasons of food production but we are now. We're not fancy chefs but we do have the best ingredients and we love to cook. This dinner is one of the best meals of our lives and we'll repeat the experience often. Perhaps we'll replace the filets with lamb, pasture-raised rabbit or Ossabaw pork tenderloin, but it will be incredible nevertheless.

There are any number of things that I could be thinking as I savor my last bite, but thinking that I have sacrificed something is definitely a thought that does not enter my consciousness. For we have sacrificed nothing but gained everything. It's simply a matter of perspective.

The reality is however, that we have sacrificed, at least based on the way many people think about it. Except on rare occasions we don't have the time or money to eat out at fancy restaurants, but perhaps you can see why we don't feel like we're missing too much. And for the most part travel is out of the question, but this is just as much due to due to lack of interest as it is financial and time constraints. We just don't want to leave the farm. When we moved here we didn't know we would grow to feel this way but feel this way we do. I feel no stress on the farm but if you want to change that, tell me that I must drive to an airport and fly away. I'm a farmer, not a jet-setter, and my place is here.

What about other sacrifices? Let's see—where did we used to spend our time and money? Golf is gone and as any golfer can tell you, between clubs, travels, balls, and greens fees or memberships, the game can cost a *lot*. It also takes an enormous amount of time, so I've saved that time and money. But more surprisingly I've lost all interest in golf, an astonishing realization for someone who, in school, played over two hundred rounds per year and almost pursued a career in the game.

Concert tickets too are gone except on very rare occasions. In the past four years we've seen one show. One of our initial criterion in finding property was to be within three hours of Atlanta. Now that we're here we find that we just have no interest in ever going there for games, concerts or events. I could say we are sacrificing but a more accurate description would be that the desire for urban stimulation has simply dissipated.

Largely out of necessity we've drastically lowered our food and living expenses and can provide most of what we need, other than paper products, foil, and the like. We can make or grow our own soaps, shampoos, butter, lard, meat, sausages, grains, cheeses, mushrooms, vegetables, and fruit for the year. I find myself not getting haircuts often enough and looking somewhat scruffy most of the time, but when I do it's at the local shop for a fraction of what I used to pay. It looks it too, but who's looking? The cows don't care and we're living our dream.

From the endless questions and comments we receive on our farm tours I know that our life of farming in the country is a dream that is shared by many. For most it's just a fantasy that they can indulge in by visiting farms like ours or following us online. Then there are others who truly endeavor to pry themselves from their urban cubicles as we did so that they can live off the land and perhaps produce enough food for others to pay the bills. They dream of living in the country but just aren't sure how to get there. It's not easy and pursuing dreams never is. That's why they are called dreams.

Tantalizingly elusive, dreams are more than something most people actually aspire to. Instead, they more closely resemble something that is "wished" for. Something that one wishes would magically "happen" to them. They are talked about for a long time and thought about for a long time, but far too often they stay just that—dreams. For a dream to become reality rather than remaining a wish the dream must morph into a personal vision. Whereas a dream can creep into my self-consciousness on its own, I on the other hand become the architect of a vision. At this point it's really no longer an abstract dream, semantics aside, but a vision that I see for myself. My vision. The question becomes whether I can make that vision a reality. I must take action by defining a series of measurable steps to do just that. If I can't, I am content to leave the dream in the fantasy category. In my experience it is at precisely this point that most people's dreams get stuck. All gung ho, they move from the dream state into a state of frenzied research, reading everything, asking everyone and endeavoring to learn everything they can about their objective so that they can make the "right" decision. They persist in a perpetual state of "almost ready" as they enter a lasting phase of paralysis by analysis. They never act on their vision beyond that. Over time the failure to act on the vision may be rationalized as they didn't have the money, or the time, or the experience, or there were competing priorities such as kids, a mortgage and so on that precluded them from doing so. They repeat tomorrow what they did today. And it's understandable why they do this—it's comfortable.

For us to become farmers we had to step way out of our comfort zone and adjust some priorities. It's as simple and utterly complex as that. Of course none of us like hearing something as simplistic (and inconsiderate) as "It's simple, all you have to do is DO IT!" Easy for them to say. Yet isn't there some truth to it? While we all may have different abilities we also each have the opportunity to manufacture a vision for ourselves that is within our own ability. It seems to me that making a dream come true takes hard work, luck, timing, planning and the assumption of risk. Ask any pro athlete if their dream came true and they may agree that it did. Then ask them how hard they worked to get there.

If your dream is to move to the country and become a farmer or homesteader, then perhaps you can make your dream come true. But as the saying goes, be careful what you wish for. The days of pastoral beauty sought by so many are indeed real and will connect you in a spiritual way with your sense of place and purpose in the world. But that connection is permanent in the sense that, at least with livestock, you can't get off the land even when you want to. If you choose this path you'll learn, as we have, the realities of the cycle of all life commencing with birth and ending with death, often prematurely and sometimes at your hand. You'll become acquainted with the changing seasons and you'll morph into your natural environment. Will this be what you want? That will be up to you.

How do we feel about having morphed into our natural world? Let me put it this way. There's an automatic red gate at the opening of the farm, a barricade of sorts that keeps the farm and its inhabitants *in* and everything else *out*. It locks in the death and drama along with the birth, hope and beauty, all of which comprise our natural world, and we cannot have one without the other. It divides our private life from our public life when we conduct tours, make deliveries or if we have to venture out into the wild—like to run to Elberton. After we've kindly shown a TV crew or reporter around the farm and they inch down the driveway the phrase you'll most often hear Liz, Amanda or I shout across the pasture to one another is "*Shut the red gate!*"

Yes, we love it out here!

⚘

I near the completion of this book with Christmas day having just passed, a fact that has caused me to reflect on how we have changed, or how farming has changed us in the four years since we found this land and went AWOL from corporate America and suburbia. The manner in which we celebrated Christmas and spent our time on the farm this year illustrates perfectly how our life has changed and is now so much richer than ever before. Prior to farming, Liz and I loved Christmas and would sometimes start opening gifts a week in advance. That's because we bought each other so many gifts we could start a week early and still have some on Christmas day. Oh, they weren't extravagant by any means—I think the first gift Liz ever gave me was a wrapped box of Fruity Pebbles. But right there, that's it. I would never eat a box of sweetened cereal like that today for too many reasons to recount here, opting instead to simply sweeten oatmeal with honey that we harvested ourselves. Then I was but a naïve consumer. Today I have become an informed and much more conscientious producer and consumer.

This year for two reasons Liz and I chose to not buy each other any gifts. For one we simply can't afford indulgences any longer, even if it's a small gift. If we don't need it, it likely won't find it's way into our home. Secondly, there's no need to buy gifts when you can make something far more special for the one you love. In the past I would rely on marketers to plant a seed in my subconscious of small, clever stocking stuffers that I could simply buy and Liz could simply forget the next day. I mean how many people remember what was in their stocking last year, or the year before? Weaning myself from the marketers this year I endeavored to fill Liz's stocking with an assortment of gourmet treats from my heart and made by my hands. Not simply a chocolate bar cleverly displayed to snag my attention in a checkout line. But something special from me to her.

She awoke to find her stocking filled with impossibly airy and flavorful marshmallows that I made from scratch, the first she had ever tasted. If you've never tasted a real, homemade marshmallow, go make yourself a batch as soon as you put this book down. You deserve it and you'll find the bagged variety isn't worthy of the name. For us, along with many other food items we gave up purchasing long ago, marshmallows will now join that list, having tasted something that is so wonderful it may be sinful. The marshmallows snuggled in her stocking next to dark chocolate pretzels and rum balls, both of which I also made from scratch. Together the trio beautifully filled Liz's stocking once they were tastefully wrapped, and brought to mind the Christmases we've all read about long ago when finding concoctions like these in your stocking was truly a special treat.

For the big present under the tree, I cut branches while pruning willow and Chinaberry trees and built a rustic table for Liz, knowing that she has become increasingly interested in the past year at doing anything and everything off the land. It wasn't a great table and you won't be seeing it on the cover of a glossy magazine. But it came from my land, my heart and my hands, and was a gift from me to her and not a gift from a department store. Along the same lines the final gift to Liz was simply a card from me, redeemable for a date to make a willow rocking chair together. This gift along with the table and stocking stuffers cost next to nothing and required the only gift she wanted anyway—my time.

For her part Liz treated me to three one-of-a-kind gifts that touched my heart. She handcrafted a walking stick from one of our sycamore tree branches, cut it to just the right height for me and engraved an endearing message along the side. This will be a handy treasure for the rest of my life as I walk the farm, herd animals and occasionally need balance chasing naughty pigs through the woods.

The second eye-popping gift was a set of four hand-made place mats. On each of them, she hand painted a different animal species, showing the common primal butcher cuts and dotted lines for each. We not only have our farm outside, we increasingly are bringing it into our home, as I now have a cow, pig, sheep and chicken placemat adorning our table.

To complete the hat trick Liz actually knitted me socks. Yes, here in the twenty-first century, we find ourselves going back in time as Liz, who knew nothing about knitting only two months prior, has become somewhat obsessed with the craft, knitting gifts for both me and her parents this Christmas. Granted, her gifts cost a few dollars in craft supplies, but it was her thoughtfulness and her skill with illustration that made it uniquely personal and unforgettable.

For Christmas dinner we enjoyed a roasted goose that would even make Ebenezer Scrooge proud. Only unlike Scrooge, or me prior to farming, we raised this goose from hatching before Liz and I butchered it together for our Christmas dinner. As the goose was roasting and I had the giblets in the pot preparing to make gravy, it occurred to me that I now know what I am looking at when I open a bag of giblets. Gizzard, liver, heart, neck. Unlike four years ago, now I know what they look like inside the *pot* and I know what they look like inside the *bird*. More importantly I know and care where they came from, what the goose ate and how she was treated. I know everything about this meal, which transcends it to a level beyond mere food to something I have a unique connection to.

With the goose browning nicely and me having a few moments to spare, I used that time to cure a side of pork belly so that we could enjoy bacon the next week. In the past if I wanted bacon next week I would run to the store next week. Today I know I have to plan it out but it's worth it. Making bacon is one of those liberating acts that once we learned how easy and how far superior it was, we never buy store-bought bacon. Students who attend our charcuterie classes on farm universally agree and join us in making all kinds of cured meats that they previously deemed beyond their reach, such as corned beef, pepperoni, salami and sausages. They leave the farm liberated, empowered and enriched, not to mention well fed.

After dinner Liz placed the goose carcass in a large pot, covered it with water, added some aromatics and let it simmer for hours. Four years ago we would buy either chicken or beef stock from a grocery store, believing these were the only two types available and never, ever thinking to make it ourselves. Today we always make stock from every carcass and would never let one go to waste. On our shelves and in our freezer, we routinely keep beef, duck, goose, turkey, chicken, venison, rabbit and even pork stock.

Still, even though we grew much of what we needed to sustain us for Christmas dinner, I bought rice for the stuffing, as I haven't gotten around to putting in our rice paddy. Yet. I also needed powdered sugar for the marshmallows, dark chocolate and, last but certainly not least, rum. So while we've really connected with where our food comes from and what it takes to produce it, we haven't gone off the deep end. We seek to not only produce as much as we require off the land, but to also make use of everything on the land, including every part of every animal. Beyond that when we want something from the store we get it. Yes, this includes the occasional soda that Liz's body craves even after a gradual four-year weaning in the country, although the need has eroded to a faint heartbeat today.

Both Liz and I were eager for Christmas to get here so that we could savor a wonderful day together. It was truly a special, memorable Christmas, and yet no animal on the farm shared our enthusiasm for the holiday. Businesses and schools, like the ones we labored at in the past, would close for all major holidays. On the farm, Christmas means nothing more to livestock than does Labor Day, Memorial Day or Thanksgiving. And so even though Christmas bells rang, chores had to be done.

After indulging on marshmallows this Christmas day, I relocated a hay ring from one paddock to another, and then took three rolls of hay each on a half-mile ride to feed cows and sheep. Driving the tractor leisurely and not feeling rushed, I simply marveled at the beauty of everything around me. With the cows waiting patiently I cut the twine that bound the hay, giving little thought to a black insect resting on the twine as I brushed it aside. It was difficult to identify without my glasses, but as it rolled over the red hourglass on its abdomen revealed her identity as a black widow spider. With venom that is excruciatingly painful and even fatal, I reflected on how many times we've had our hand on or near these spiders since we began farming. Perched underneath spigots, resting near the handle of step-in posts or lounging on garden tools, they share our habitat in large numbers, a fact we'd probably prefer wasn't true but it is and we accept it.

After hay was doled out, the rare breed American Chinchilla rabbits, two of which had just kindled babies, needed checking on. Perhaps owing to their thick, luxurious silver fur, they seemed happier than ever in the cold. Hens and turkeys wanted breakfast, pigs needed to be checked on, roost bars had to be put down in the morning and then put back up in the evening with the collection and cleaning of eggs. All in all a very light day of chores compared to our busy season, but still enough that we couldn't escape the farm had we wished to. We didn't. Liz called Amanda, our wonderful on-farm apprentice who has become like family to us, and together they used the extra time to concoct myriad soaps, lotions and shampoos.

As light faded, snow began to fall, blanketing us Dixie farmers with a white Christmas. In the three years we've lived on this land, it has snowed measurably at least once each year. When the snow has fallen and the winds are calm, we walk the farm, relishing in how quiet and peaceful everything is. We stroll, hold hands and embrace the serene tranquility of our world. With nowhere to go, no traffic to fight and, generally not remotely sure what day it is, it feels to us as if we are alone with our animals in a most beautiful and intimate snow globe.

With sunrise the following morning, I awoke to do my share of the chores knowing that Liz and Amanda would also be doing theirs. It mattered not in the least to the pigs that it was the day after Christmas. It only mattered that they were fed. A cold, bitter wind whipped my face as I cranked the tractor and carried the twenty 50-pound bags of feed I had just hoisted into the loader bucket on the front of the tractor. Stopping the tractor just short of their electric fence and with the bucket raised to the top of their feeder, about seven feet high, I shimmied my aging body over the icy hood, holding onto the loader arms for support, and climbed into the bucket. Once there I tore open each bag and to the pig's audible delight dumped them into the one-ton feeder. The bitter cold made my fingers throb with pain due to the arthritis that has taken hold in recent years. It's harder to grip now than it used to be and opening the bags requires a tight grip. Anytime it gets cold, as any arthritis sufferer will tell you, it can become excruciating. The pigs showed no concern about this either.

I'll thank my mom for the gift of arthritis, no doubt a debt she owes to her mother for hers. In years past I could have stayed in bed for the holidays or watched football, keeping my fingers warm and my body comfortable. Then again, like a growing number of people, I had surgery to remove carpel tunnel a few years ago, thanks to years on a computer, so I suppose painful fingers can be a burden with any number of jobs. The arthritis never stopped my mother or grandmother from working and providing for those in their care, and it won't deter me.

Beyond the obvious chores there were the things not to *do*, but to *fret about*. Our walk-in freezer, which holds our entire inventory of frozen meats, stopped working on Christmas Eve, a Friday. This meant that I could do nothing to repair it until Monday after Christmas, and so I checked it constantly to ensure the temperature in the freezer hovered below freezing. As we enjoyed Christmas dinner I silently sweated over the potential freezer fiasco while Liz and Amanda worried about a lamb that had just been born in the snow, tiny piglets that were fumbling around in their mother's nest, and a sick calf lying in a bed of hay. In my mind the calculator clicked on— automatically and uninvited, as always—figuring the value of the inventory and measuring that against the repair cost, which I was told would exceed $4,000. This is on top of the $9,000 we spent last year repairing freezers. It is these types of never-ending "one-time" expenses that make profitable farming very, very elusive.

Such is the farming life and such is the new life we chose for ourselves in the country. Enduring unending worry and never-ending chores in exchange for living a life completely in harmony with nature and enjoying near utter independence. Our needs have declined remarkably, not only because we can produce so much of what we need but also because we find we now crave so much less than we used to. We have become humbled, grateful and keenly aware of what we *truly* need and what it takes to really provide us with that. We find that we just don't need as much. A blissful, perfect day for us, any and every day, is a leisurely stroll around our land adoring, cultivating and harvesting the treasures of nature. We want for nothing more.

It's the little, almost indescribable things we embrace that cost so little yet enrich us so. Like stripping bark off willow branches to weave a basket. Pruning fruit trees and grape vines and using their wood for smoking meats or making crafts while laying the groundwork for a cornucopia of fruit the following year. Picking and preserving berries, tanning hides to make leather, dry curing sausages, taking a hot loaf of bread out of the oven and smearing it with fresh butter from raw milk, which we made, of course. Or sitting on the grass in the middle of a cow paddock and listening to the almost deafening sound of an orchestra of cows tearing lush spring grass from the ground and doing the one thing they both evolved and long to do.

And of course, bottle-feeding a baby lamb that was harshly rejected by its mother and placing it snugly in a container at our feet as we watch TV, giving the lamb what it needs to survive while medicating the pink and blue flu that has infected us, once again. It's not a child, but it's something to care for.

Then again, as Liz is all too apt to remind me when we're stressed and overwhelmed, we could have all that harmony and independence for ourselves by simply homesteading and not farming commercially. Like when we have $4,000 freezer repair bills. So each year we ask ourselves why we're working so hard as we seek ways to tweak our approach, hoping to eliminate just enough of the stress so that we can take back our time and enjoy the life we moved out here for. With each passing year, we find ourselves less inspired to simply maximize food production per acre and more motivated to empower and liberate others through educational and agritourism events, allowing consumers to genuinely reconnect with their food. Events like classes on butchering, cheese making, charcuterie, and even hide tanning. Rustic farm stays and dinners where consumers can reconnect with the animals and the land in the very real way that we do, if only for a brief respite. These events are no less work for us but they do keep us on the farm instead of being at farmers markets or on deliveries, while still giving us time with interested and compassionate consumers. We love sharing our farm with others but the farm is here, not on an asphalt surface at the farmers market.

We will continue to seek this balance between enjoying the life we crave and giving loyal customers as much of our farm and what it produces as they crave. Still, the farm will endure and produce as much food as we can comfortably manage. Regardless of the financial obstacles and the stress, there's no way I can stop farming. For I am a farmer.

The animals on our farm are now diverse and many, with over fifty cows, one hundred pigs, scores of sheep, and thousands of poultry talons scratching the ground. Each animal was born on our farm and each passing generation grows stronger, happier and healthier, regaining his or her ability to completely thrive in a natural environment. Our land needs to be nourished by these animals, and for the land, I will farm.

The animals need to be reconnected with nature and continue redeveloping the maternal traits and hardiness that mankind stole from them. So for these animals and the health of their future generations, I will farm.

The community of people who count on us need the nourishment provided by the animals and they deserve complete transparency into how their food is produced. We count on them and they can count on us. So, for these caring consumers and dear friends, I will farm.

For the future farmers who need inspiration, encouragement and on-the-job training via our events or apprentice program, and who will also need hardy breeds of animals in order to realize their own farm dreams, I will farm.

And for society as a whole, which would be well served to have a more profound respect for the soil and the rules of nature, I will farm.

Still our path was not the easiest choice and has required us to develop a different perspective and adapt a different set of expectations from our urban rearing. By a wide margin this is the worst-paying job I have ever had. By an equally wide margin it is also the most rewarding. After decades of my searching hopelessly in vain, my calling finally found me. I am so deeply thankful that it did.

I cannot change the fact that I was not born a farmer. But, indeed, I was born to farm.

The End

Book Club and Reading Group Guide
The Accidental Farmers

Questions and Topics for Discussion

1. If you reflect on your own cooking and eating habits as author Tim Young did, what would you conclude about your life?

2. In the prologue Young asked, "Are we all working hard to earn money to pay for food, housing and other things that, if we weren't working so hard, we could grow, build and provide for ourselves?" How would you respond to this?

3. If you moved to a very rural area as the Youngs did, what would be the most difficult things for you to give up?

4. Young believes that cows and sheep should be allowed to consume only grass, which they have evolved to eat, because he views it as healthier and biologically sustainable. Yet this model makes food appear more expensive since it takes animals longer to grow and they produce less milk. Do you agree with his view, and could you re-prioritize your spending to support this type of food production?

5. If a young man wishes to become a life-saving doctor, he must invest a large sum in education and then work for years to become highly skilled in his profession. To become a life-nourishing farmer, he must invest an equally large sum in land and equipment and then work for years to

become highly skilled in his profession. Do you believe society recognizes doctors and farmers equally in terms of financial and social rewards? Should they?

6. Young described how he and his wife almost had to surrender their farm dreams due to her allergic reaction on the farm. He goes on to suggest that humanity's pursuit of a climate-controlled and sterile world likely contributed to an overall increase in allergies. Do you agree? If we continue on this path, a hundred years from now what might our relationship to allergens be like ?

7. Some people believe that consumers should have the right to buy raw milk or a processed chicken directly from a farmer, while others believe that strict food safety laws are required, even though they may result in such foods being deemed unsafe. Where should we draw the line when it comes to consumers' right to free choice and the public's need for a safe food system?

8. Young questions what is more humane—leaving a sick animal to suffer while giving it the opportunity to recover, or shooting the animal and denying it that opportunity. What is your opinion? If you conclude that a cow should be put down, could you do it?

9. In the chapter "Eating Animals," Young asks, "Who are the real animal rights supporters...the ones who aspire to deny life (animal rights activists) or the ones who aspire to grant each animal a natural life that will ultimately end (farmers)?" What do you think?

10. Young stated that a person with the financial resources to acquire enough land to farm livestock would achieve a better return through other business ventures. If a person is interested in sustainable farming, how can they possibly hope to obtain land? Is this a public or private issue?

11. Young described how he and his wife have had to learn many lost arts such as canning, cheese making, animal husbandry, butchering, hide tanning, soap making, charcuterie and more. What lost art skills appeal to you the most?

12. How have your views and visual images of natural farming changed after reading this book?

13. Young feels strongly that male pigs should not be subjected to castration, as it is unnecessary and painful. How would you go about changing consumers' expectations about how a boar may taste different than a sow, just as a doe deer tastes different than a buck?

14. If you were a livestock farmer, where would you draw the line between providing support to the animals vs. letting nature take its course?

15. How has this book changed the way you think about farming and food production?

16. If the book inspired you to support small family farms, what are some of the first steps you will take to make a change in how you buy food?

Endnotes

1 http://quarriesandbeyond.org/articles_and_books/elberton_granite_indus_flourishes.html
2 Our experience at Nature's Harmony Farm
3 http://www.thepigsite.com/articles/15/genetics/3245/managing-boar-taint-focus-on-genetic-markers
4 Squires, 1999
5 http://www.ciwf.org.uk/what_we_do/pigs/state_of_eu_pigs/pig_welfare_explained.aspx
6 http://www.thepigsite.com/articles/1/pig-health-and-welfare/2137/castration-of-pigs
7 http://www2.mcdaniel.edu/Biology/wildamerica/grasslands/graslandoutline.html
8 Voisin, Grass Productivity, pg 115
9 http://cattletoday.info/grasstetany.htm
10 http://www.thebeefsite.com/diseaseinfo/223/nitrate-poisoning
11 http://www.loc.gov/rr/scitech/mysteries/smallestflower.html
12 http://science-in-farming.library4farming.org/Seeds_1/LIFE-PROCESSES-OF-SEEDS/How-Long-Can-a-Seed-Remain-Alive.html
13 http://biology.clc.uc.edu/fankhauser/cheese/rennet/rennet.html
14 Singer, Peter, Animal Liberation, 1975, p. 123.

LaVergne, TN USA
18 February 2011
217046LV00001B/32/P